FROM CAMPUS
TO CORNER OFFICE

HOW CO-OPS AND INTERNSHIPS WILL HELP YOU WIN
IN THE WORKPLACE!

CURTIS L. ODOM, ED.D.

Book•nol•o•gy
n. delivering useable information and knowledge
that adds value to people's lives

A BUSINESS & EDUCATIONAL IMPRINT FROM ADDUCENT
WWW.ADDUCENTINC.COM

TITLES DISTRIBUTED IN
NORTH AMERICA
UNITED KINGDOM
WESTERN EUROPE
SOUTH AMERICA
AUSTRALIA
CHINA
INDIA

From Campus to Corner Office

How Co-Ops and Internships Will Help You Win in the Workplace!

Curtis L. Odom, Ed.D.

FIRST EDITION

PAPERBACK ISBN: 9781937592790

PUBLISHED BY BOOKNOLOGY (A BUSINESS AND EDUCATIONAL IMPRINT FROM ADDUCENT)

JACKSONVILLE, FLORIDA

WWW.ADDUCENTINC.COM

DEDICATION

To my professor, dissertation chair, coach, mentor, friend, and professorial role model, Dr. John 'Jack' McManus. Your steady support and belief in me through four years chasing my doctorate at Pepperdine University were invaluable. Thank you for encouraging me to reach my goal of becoming full-time faculty at a business school in Boston. Your teaching me to 'pay it forward' became my mantra. And that has brought me joy that only comes from having discovered that my purpose is to inspire others to live an abundant, fearless, and grateful life.

Go Red Sox!

ACKNOWLEDGMENTS

To my beautiful wife and best friend for life, Nelia. You are my creative muse. I am again reminded that there is no 'me' without you. As we start yet another chapter in our incredible story, your willingness to always listen continues to inspire me. This book, my 4th, is yet another dream that took shape as an idea, which turned into months of early mornings and late nights as I went about the work of writing it. You are my reason for everything. Your fingerprints are on my every success. I cannot imagine this world without you to share every experience. Your love for me is the song in my heart. I love you!

To my lovely daughter and best giggle buddy, Alyssa. I've watched you grow from an adorable little girl into a charming and lovely young lady. And every day I am prouder of you. It is a blessing and a privilege to have you as my daughter. We are so much alike, in so many ways. I aspire daily to be your hero, to be your role model for the type of leader I hope you will one day become. I hope this book will remind you one day, long after I am gone, that your Dad took the greatest joys of his life from the moments spent looking at the world through your smiling eyes while sitting next to you at sunset on a beach. I love you!

To Strive, To Seek, To Find, and Not To Yield - Tennyson

TABLE OF CONTENTS

Introduction

The Corner Office as a Metaphor

For many, our physical offices are both a reflection and an extension of our personalities. But our generationally dynamic workforce has changed in ways that are challenging the workplace to also change. The concept of the workplace must be rethought and redesigned for the current workforce. To reflect not only who we are, but also how we work. In the gig economy, the corner office has been traded in for mobility.

To identify how we got here, we need a short history lesson.

In the period immediately following World War II, the workplace was singular-minded. Everyone had their own space isolated from others where they worked. Even inter-office communication came through memos delivered by secretaries. These spaces were a reflection of 'who' you were; they were—in truth—an indication of your status in the office hierarchy. With the corner office, for many, being the ultimate goal within any organization.

How and where we work now is already in the future.

Over the years, we've changed our definition of work. In fact, 'how' we work is now the prime driver in our society. Look around you... we've entered the sharing economy where the idea of pooling resources and collaboration permeates our society from top to bottom. The future of the workplace is less focused on the physical space but rather how we work within it. Everyone's method of

1

working is different. And, with that in mind, it stands to reason that there should not be a singular model of the workplace to follow. Instead, the workplace should be focused on zones that provide distinct areas that genuinely reflect how attentively you work. In the context of 'how' we work, attention is the most important thing. At the end of the day, the best work will not come from the best office, but rather from how you work in the space you have. That is the future of the modern workplace.

Welcome to the corner office of today.

The pendulum has swung from one end—offices with closed doors and rows of cubes, to the other—wide-open workspaces where employees find themselves more easily distracted and less productive. And now, the idea of the corner office is a metaphor for being in the best position to be in charge of your career goals. This way of thinking—when applied—is paying dividends in this new environment. Those organizations and professionals that can flexibly and nimbly adapt to the growing needs of the modern workforce— where collaboration becomes a way of life, and not just something you do in a conference room—have a distinct advantage.

The physical corner office for the modern workforce has changed. The corner office is any workplace or even public place where today's workforce can find themselves feel welcomed, valued, able to contribute and to be their authentic self.

THE ASSESSMENT

There is an initial transaction between someone applying for a position and their prospective employer (the company looking to fill the position). And it involves something that many people are uncomfortable with. But in the job market (and in the career climb) you need to know how to position and present yourself, i.e., 'sell yourself.' This is especially important in today's business environment.

The best way to sell yourself is being prepared, and in many ways, that alone does the selling for you. It's self-promotion by preparation. That's one of the key things I share with those who ask for my advice. This simple effort separates the men from the boys and the women from the girls.

If you know the role you want and you've looked at all that you have to do or the experiences you need to have, and say, I don't want to do it. Well, you just told yourself (and others) everything needed to know about yourself. That you really don't want the opportunity. You want the trappings. You want the rewards. You want the title. But you aren't prepared to do the work it takes to get there. And you know what? That's not a comfortable conversation for someone to have (even with themselves), but it's one of the most critical discussions in your career.

It's easier to get what you want in life if you are brutally honest enough to understand who you are from the beginning. If you don't feel like you're ready or don't want to do all that it would take to reach your aspirations, then don't do it. But more importantly, don't whine, cry, complain, and moan when you don't get to that level if you know deep down in your heart of hearts you haven't done everything it takes to succeed to the extent that you hoped for.

We are not talking about entering a popularity contest to reach high levels of executive management. Yes, popularity and personal charisma are important, but at the end of the day, it all boils down to your resume in front of the hiring manager or the decision maker.

What about your resume stands out?

What does your resume lack that they are looking for?

One goal I have to share with you is this. I always set myself up so that whenever my resume was in the hands of a decision maker, I never wanted them to think, "Wow! This candidate would be perfect for us if he only had _____." I've taken care of that. There is no 'if he only had.' Perhaps the strategy that I employed to my success could work for you too? Ask yourself, what do I need on my resume for the role I'm looking for with a company? Better yet, what things should be on it that will make them say to themselves, 'We have to talk to this person ... their background and experience are perfect for this position.'

I've worked in multiple industries in positions of increasing levels of difficulty and seniority, building my career step-by-step. It has taken many personal sacrifices, a lot of time, and plenty of money to be able to do that. But if you're going to compete for the top positions, you've got to be exemplary, you've got to be extraordinary, and a lot goes into that. Not only in work needed to strengthen your resume but also in networking to make the right contacts that will help you in your career. I never lost sight of the fact that the resume I had built was only to get me the interview. It is up to me once in the interview to sell myself so well that I would get the job. And, I have been smart enough to never turn down a job interview ... and wise enough to not accept every job offer. In short, I have followed the very advice that I am giving you in this book to go from campus to the corner office.

WHERE TO FOCUS

The Importance of Experience

There's a difference between studying hard and working hard. Many graduating college seniors believe that grades are all that matter for admission to graduate school or to land a good entry-level job. I'm here to tell you that thinking is dead wrong. In fact, colleges are the first to say that you need more than a degree to get hired.

As a former hiring manager and current business school professor, I can confirm that a candidate or potential new hire with work experience is more attractive than those without.

Many ambitious young adults disrespect the value of work experience because they've had jobs that have no connection to their future plans — and pay poorly.

But working anywhere can teach you many valuable lessons, even if your job isn't intellectually challenging. Try to find employment in a field you're interested in, even if the job itself seems like a dead-end.

The current job market has created a demand for those who have paid internships or structured cooperative learning (co-op) work experience while in school. So, job candidates with that experience rise to the top. That is why such experience is now an essential graduation requirement. Learning more about the industry you're interested in, gaining experience, is something that not only impresses a potential employer... it helps you discover your own strengths and weaknesses. Many college students find their chosen industry so compelling that an internship or co-op cements their college major and career decision. Some, however, find the industry so boring that their experience leads them to change their career plans. But it's better to learn that lesson during a one-semester internship, or six-month co-op than after a full year or more as a full-time employee.

Performing well as an intern or co-op can also lead you to the next step in the industry. Your manager may write you a recommendation for graduate school or for a better internship. You could even get a full-time job offer or a job lead from a co-worker who was impressed

5

by your work. Plus, interning can give you a chance to learn what your best job skills are, which skills need improvement and how to work with people. Many ambitious young people think that lower-level jobs are an impediment to success because they're time-consuming and cause employers to stereotype you as someone with lower-level skills.

Some students choose to delay the world of work by pursuing a master's degree only to be advised by college career offices and graduate admissions offices to work full-time for a few years after graduating college. Why? Because professional experience is essential, and because much of a Master of Business Administration (MBA) program coursework analyzes everyday business problems. Students who make the jump without work experience are less competitive for employment when they finish their degrees than their classmates with work experience.

Colleges aren't the only ones weighing in. Even future employers in a variety of fields feel that real-world experience is the only thing standing between some graduates and their dream jobs. Whether it is a paid or volunteer status, this involvement [in your desired field] will increase [your] confidence and savvy while exhibiting dedication and responsibility. This comes down to many employers believing that a person should focus on what they are good at and what they enjoy.

Finding the right placement can be tricky, but if it is planned in advance, taking into account the distance you will have to travel, and the type of company you want to work for will have a significant impact on your experience. Therefore it is vital to get it right from the start!

Work experience should be related to your course and the industry you want to work in as a career. The list of possibilities are endless, it's up to you to find the one that fits you best! Wherever you decide to go, your work experience should be meaningful and with a purpose. Don't underestimate yourself or your ability. You will have skills to offer the right organization. Take the time to write down the things you are good at and the things you enjoy doing. The one thing to remember is this is *your* work experience, and it has to be right for you! And work experience builds self-esteem and makes you a valued person in the community. There is a vast range of benefits to having tailored your professional expertise.

Your internship or co-op experience should be structured to provide learning that is purposeful, substantial, offer challenge and be relevant to your study program and career aspirations. It should have a structured plan for the duration of the placement, should focus on the skills required for that area, and be followed up by some form of reference/feedback from the employer based on performance. You will not become a managing director on your first day! You will often be given tasks that you think are not relevant. However, every opportunity is a chance to learn. You will often be working alongside people who have been on the job for years, and they may be willing be able to pass their knowledge on to you ... but only if you ask.

Ideally, placements should be with an organization closely matching what you are studying, but some areas of work are difficult to find internships in due to health and safety. In these instances, the college will look to find a close match. For example, it is hard to place a 22-year-old on a construction site. So placement with a builder's merchant would be acceptable. You may be required to complete a log book when on placement as many of the skills you will gain during the placement can be put onto your resume for future use in looking for a job/apprenticeship.

Work experience is a taste of the world of work. You will get your first in the professional workforce. Do you know what you want to do? It's the best way to get a real sense of your chosen industry and to check that it is definitely something you want to pursue. Do you not know that you want to do it? It's a great way to test a job that you think you might like to do out but without committing. Work experience—if it resonates with you—also shows passion and interest to future employers. It proves that you are motivated to get into a chosen career and that you've done your homework.

Internships

Your most useful source of work experience may not be one that pays well or at all. Begin looking for internship opportunities early in your college career—the summer after freshman or sophomore year, for example. To find internships, visit your college career center, as well as online resources such as Internships.com and Idealist (for targeted nonprofit opportunities). Locating the right internship can be challenging, so be sure to do your research before you decide to pursue the opportunity.

The benefit of completing an internship is its focus on educating you on the inner workings of a particular field or business. Interns are expected to be learning, as well as contributing. The downside of an internship is its low or non-existent pay. In the past few years, the role of the intern has shifted dramatically as a result of the gig economy.

According to the Bureau of Labor and Statistics, there is no official definition of the 'gig economy'—or, for that matter, a gig. For purposes of this book, a gig describes a single project or task for which a worker is hired, often through a digital marketplace, to work on demand. Some gigs are a type of short-term job, and some workers pursue them as a self—employment option. Those concepts are not new. However, companies connecting workers with these jobs through websites or mobile applications (more commonly known as apps) are a more recent development.

Gig workers are spread among diverse occupation groups and are not easily identified in surveys of employment and earnings. But they are similar in the way they earn money. Gig workers often get gigs using a website or mobile app that helps to match them with customers. Some gigs may be very brief, such as answering a 5--minute survey. Others are much longer in duration, such as an 18—month database management project. And when one gig is over, workers who earn a steady income this way must find another. So this sometimes means juggling multiple jobs at once.

The employer mindset has gone from viewing the internship as a form of corporate community service, to a method for accessing free labor. In a thriving economy, companies want to invest in the future workforce by providing opportunities for young emerging professionals to learn about their industry and professions. However, when times get tough, employers want to simply stay alive long enough to get through the recession.

As an intern, you will need to adjust to this new gig mindset and approach internships differently than in the past. Instead of approaching it as an opportunity to learn about a profession or industry, you'll want to pursue an internship with the goal of contributing your skills in a way that generates value and substance for the employer. As a result of your contribution, you will no doubt learn about your profession and industry, but your goal should be contributing not learning. Businesses are trying to make their dollars go further, and their people produce more. Internships help them accomplish both. Promoting yourself as the intern who can assist them do more for less is a great way to get noticed.

So, what does this mean for you? Well for starters, when asked in an interview, "Why do you want this internship?" focus on what you can do for the employer. Do not focus on talking about how this is a great opportunity for you to learn about the industry and profession. Talk more about what you can bring to the employer or the organization. This is now the most important reason to highlight in the interview. What's valuable to the employer is your ability to take the initiative and produce quality work as a member of their team. In other words, what does the organization get for bringing you onboard?

Plan Your Career Path

While career plans may not be at the forefront of your mind during your first and second years at university, early preparation can give you a significant advantage. Graduation can initially seem a long way off. Inevitably, making the most of your time at college is a higher priority than thinking about what job you'd like to do when it's over. However, doing some research at this stage will make the process much easier in the long run—and help you to avoid the panic that can set in for those who leave university with no idea of their next move.

Career planning is as much about understanding yourself as it is about exploring opportunities and there are many ways in which you can develop your skills and experience to help make informed career choices. Many students make very little use of their university's career services office until they are nearing the end of their final semester, but engagement is the key to getting ahead. Find out what support is available and make use of it. In addition to appointments and workshops, career services office often run employer and sector events throughout the academic year, such as careers fairs, industry insights, and employer talks.

There are two sides to career planning at this stage. The first is deciding the career path you want to follow. The second is ensuring that you have the skills and experience—alongside your academic achievements—to impress employers. Set yourself goals for each academic year to make the most of opportunities, so you have a plan in place for your final year. Not only will early career planning give you time to explore job options, but it can also help you to develop the skills and experience you'll need for a fruitful and fulfilling career.

Seek Out Opportunities

You'll find it much easier to build a formidable resume over the years than by reaching the end of your final semester before realizing you don't meet the entry requirements for your chosen job. In your first year start generating ideas and undertake research into the job market. Getting involved in extracurricular activities, such as joining societies, peer mentoring, being a student ambassador and volunteering, will help you develop valuable skills and experience. In your second year seek out opportunities for relevant work placements, which will help you assess what work you enjoy. If you are interested in being self-employed, use your time at university to test your business ideas and enterprise skills. By the time your third year comes around, you'll be ready to start applying for jobs or graduate programs. You will also find more helpful guidance on choosing a career.

Gaining Experience

In competitive job markets, there's a real advantage to having work experience before graduating. You may think that you're ideally suited to the job you're applying for, but if you don't have access to examples of how you've put your skills to good use, it'll be much harder to convince employers of your suitability. Almost half of those questioned said that it was either not very likely or not at all likely that a graduate without any previous work experience would be successful in the selection process, irrespective of their academic achievements. Many employers are now using work placement schemes as the first stage in their recruitment process. Many entry-level jobs are expected to be filled by graduates who have already worked for the company in some form, either through a paid internship, summer job or co-op placement. Furthermore, networking opportunities provided by professional experience will connect you with people who may be able to help progress your career.

Part of the Student Journey

It's never too early to get some work experience, with many employers offering something for those at each stage of the student journey. Nearly two-thirds of organizations offer paid internships and work placements, or open days, introductory courses and other 'try before you buy' experiences to first-year undergraduates. For instance, placements that typically last one or two weeks. You may join a specific team, be rotated around different teams or work on a group project. Whichever format is chosen, you will gain confidence, improved communication skills, and an understanding of the skills businesses are looking for in the employees they hire.

Supplementing your degree by participating in extracurricular activities is arguably as important as gaining the diploma itself. There's much more to university than studying. Lectures, essays and exams are only part of student life, and higher education provides a fantastic opportunity to experience new things. Extracurricular activities are a perfect way for a student to fully immerse themselves in the diverse and exciting student community. Here are three ways to make the most of your time at university...

Getting involved in a university club or society doesn't just create lasting memories; it also significantly increases your appeal to employers. You'll build valuable connections, meet hundreds of like-minded students from all backgrounds, and gain transferable skills such as teamwork, leadership, organization, communication, problem-solving and time management. Participation also improves your confidence. There are often many sports available. Some students take part to keep fit and play competitively, while others join in for the social life. Societies, meanwhile, come in all shapes and sizes. If nothing matches your passion, you can apply to create your own community by contacting the students' union. You should be doing the things they are interested in, not the things your friends are pressuring you into. You could boost your resume even further by becoming chairperson, secretary or treasurer of a university club, or put yourself forward as a course representative or member of the students' union.

Volunteering

Unpaid voluntary work is often undertaken with charities and nonprofit organizations such as schools, hospitals, and community centers. And it is a fantastic way to meet people outside of your university and network with potential employers. It also provides valuable work-based experience, helps you to decide on your future career, and allows you to put theory from your course into practice. What's more, research suggests that volunteering can benefit your mental health by increasing your self-esteem and a sense of purpose. You feel terrific when you do it. Before looking for opportunities, think about the type of organization that you'd like to help and what you want to achieve. Having clear aims will focus your search.

Part-time Work / Co-Op

Working and earning while at university supplements your student loan. However, part-time employment also hones many transferable skills, while demonstrating that you can cope with the conflicting demands of work and study. These skills include organization, communication, leadership, decision-making and commercial awareness. The reason why gaining and developing these skills is essential is quite simple—employers value them. Students with some form of work experience are more likely to get jobs first. Indeed, most employees are offered jobs at companies where they've gained paid work experience.

Part-Time employment also allows you to get insight into a career. This can help you to discover what you do and don't enjoy about different working environments. If a student would like to work in the finance sector, for example, getting a job as a finance assistant in a company will provide them with an insight of the role—and will also offer the opportunity. This can help you to discover what you do and don't enjoy about different working environments.

If you would like to work in the finance sector, for example, getting a job as a finance assistant in a company will provide you with insight into the role—and will also offer the opportunity to meet and network with like-minded people from an early stage. Begin your search for work at your university's careers service or students' union.

THE BURNING PLATFORM

It's no secret that college is expensive or that the high cost of obtaining a degree is *still* going up. Even worse, a large number of prospective high school students and their parents have little concept of the costs they might soon face.

In a report on a financial wellness site for teens, more than 50% of college hopefuls said they expect to graduate with just $10,000 in loans. But given that the average Class of 2016 graduate came away $37,172 in debt that estimate is pretty off the mark. In fact, only 9% of teens are willing to rack up between $20,000 and $50,000 of debt, which is far more in line with the average.

If you're in the college-planning phase, it's critical that you approach the application process with a realistic sense of what the degree you want will cost. Otherwise, you could be in for a huge amount of shock and disappointment.

The Shock of College Costs Today

Most college hopefuls know by now that getting a degree doesn't come cheap, but based on the data we've looked at, it's clear that many don't *really* know what to expect as far as costs go. So here's what tuition and fees look like, on average, for the 2017-2018 school year, according to the College Board:

- $3,570 per year for public two-year (community) colleges.
- $9,970 per year for public four-year in-state colleges.
- $25,620 per year for public four-year out-of-state colleges.
- $34,740 per year for private four-year colleges.

And these costs are just for the tuition! Throw in room and board, books, and fees... and you're looking at anywhere between $8,400 and $12,200 per year *on top of* those figures. Ouch! Now if you're lucky enough to have saved well for your education, you may be in luck. But if you're like the majority of college hopefuls out there, it'll probably be on you to fund a large chunk of your education. And that typically means one thing: loans, loans, and more loans. On the other hand, if you take steps to keep your college costs to a minimum, you'll end up less saddled with debt once you graduate and that will set the stage for a much healthier financial future.

Cutting Your College Costs

The College Board reports that it takes 12 years, on average, to recoup the cost of an undergraduate degree. That's not unrealistic, but keep in mind that this assumes you end up borrowing an average amount of money. Borrow too much, and you could end up paying back that debt until you are 50 years old. Which, incidentally, is the exact predicament nearly 40% of borrowers find themselves in. So how do you avoid this debt trap while earning your education?

To start, consult the preceding list of prices and choose the most economical degree possible. There's no need to pay a premium for a fancy private college unless you find one that happens to offer a unique program in your area of study. Choosing a public in-state school over a private one, for example, could save you close to $100,000 over a four-year period on tuition and fees alone. Another idea is to load up on credits while you're enrolled full-time to complete your degree sooner. Graduate from college a year early, and you could have that much less money to shell out over the course of your degree. But, you will also run the risk of not having an authentic college experience.

THIS BOOK TO YOUR RESCUE

And that is where this becomes your playbook. It will help you learn how to use college co-ops and internships as a cornerstone of your plan for affording the college experience. Earning while learning is quickly becoming the new method that pays financial dividends, gives you practical experience in your career field or focus... and leads to paying less in high-interest loan payments as you continue to progress to your reserved seat in the modern day corner office.

CHAPTER 1

DO YOU WANT A GUARANTEED JOB AFTER COLLEGE?

REASONS TO WANT A CO-OP OR INTERNSHIP

Let's work down the list of reasons you should consider a co-op or an internship:

1. Employers increasingly want to see experience in the new college grads they hire. A staggering 95 percent of employers said candidate experience is a factor in hiring decisions, according to an annual survey by the National Association of Colleges and Employers (NACE) Nearly half of surveyed employers wanted new-grad experience to come from internships or co-op programs. If you have completed internships, you will clearly have the edge over your classmates who haven't. In an Associated Press article, reporter Emily Fredrix quotes Philip D. Gardner, research director of the Collegiate Employment Research Institute, as saying that internship experience is "just one of those things you have to have before employers even consider looking at your resume."

2. Employers increasingly see their internship programs as the best path for hiring entry-level candidates. "Not only does participation in an internship make the student a more attractive candidate," says NACE Executive Director Marilyn Macke, "but it can also be an avenue to a job." NACE's 2016 Experiential Education Survey shows that hiring from the intern program is growing. Employers reported that nearly 36 percent of the new college graduates they hired from the Class of 2017 came from their own internship programs, up from

30 percent from the Class of 2015. Recruiting guru Dr. John Sullivan writes on the Electronic Recruiting Exchange that "the most effective sources I have worked with have consistently found that quality internship programs produce the highest quality candidates, the most productive hires, and the hires with the highest retention rates."

3. You may get paid more when you graduate if you've done one or more internships. Even back in 2015, NACE reported that surveyed employers that hired entry-level candidates with internship/co-op experience paid them 6.5 more than those without the experience.

4. You could earn college credit toward your degree. Many if not most colleges provide credit for eligible internships. Check with your faculty advisor or career-services office to see what your school's or major department's policies are.

5. Internships enable you to take your career plan for a test drive. You might discover by interning in your planned career field that it's not what you thought it would be like. Or one niche of your field is a better fit for you than another. Let's say you're a marketing major, and you complete an internship in marketing research. You discover you hate it. Before giving up on marketing, you do an internship in public relations and find it's a perfect fit for you. Isn't it better to figure all this out before you graduate and are stuck in a field that's not for you? You can also test out career paths, not in your major. Let's say you've decided on a major but always had a lingering interest in a completely different field. You could do an internship in the other field to decide how strong your interest really is and whether you want to beef up your studies in that field.

6. You'll gain valuable understanding of your major field and be better able to grasp how your coursework is preparing you to enter your chosen career. You may also discover gaps in your classroom

learning and what you need to know in the real world and can strategize how you will fill those gaps. Some employers will even suggest additional courses you should consider.

7. You'll develop skills galore. Maybe you already have the great interpersonal skills employers seek. In a co-op, you can't help but sharpen your skills by interacting with people on a professional level and in a way, that you would never have the opportunity to do in the classroom. The same goes for the teamwork, communication, leadership, and problem-solving skills that employers lust for.

8. You'll gain confidence. If you're afraid of facing the work world when you graduate, an internship will teach you that you can do it.

9. You'll build motivation and work habits. All that freedom you gained when you left home for college may have caused your motivation and work ethic to slip. You might be skipping a few classes, missing assignments, or building a class schedule that doesn't require you to get up early. There's nothing like an internship, or co-op — where you can't slack off if you want to succeed — to instill in you the workplace characteristics you'll need after you graduate.

10. You'll build your network. Everyone you meet on an internship, or co-op is a potential contact for your network and someone you can call upon for advice and referrals when you are job-hunting closer to graduation time.

11. You will build your resume. Any kind of experience on your resume is helpful, but career-relevant internship experience will make a better impression on employers than your serving job at a restaurant working for tips.

12. Growing numbers of colleges require internships. If they require them, they must be convinced that internships are important.

Similarly, studies show increasing numbers of students are completing internships. Presumably, these students know that internships are valuable for all the reasons listed here.

13. You might make some money. Not all internships are paid, of course, but those that do pay can yield pretty decent salaries. Now, you may be saying, "I know all this stuff, but insurmountable obstacles keep me from doing internships." Perhaps it's imperative that you hold a paying job that leaves no time for internships. Perhaps you have family, athletic, or extracurricular obligations. Maybe you live or attend school in an area where internships are scarce. While all these are legitimate obstacles, I still say find a way to complete at least one internship. Work with your school's career-services office to surmount your obstacles and become an intern. If other paid or unpaid obligations are the issues, target summer when your school obligations are decreased. Juggle your schedule, so you are essentially working two jobs — your internship and your other obligations. But don't overlook the possibility of internships during your time in school. If you get college credit for an internship, you can spend the time you would have spent on coursework completing your internship. Bottom line and final thought: Think creatively about how you can do an internship even if you are convinced you can't. It's that important as a step toward that corner office as you leave campus.

INTERNSHIPS

Are They Worth It?

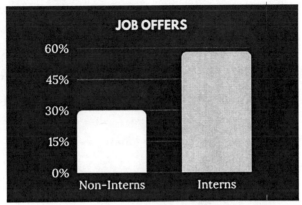

JOB OFFERS

Interns are 70% more likely to be hired as full-time employees with any company.

MEDIAN STARTING SALARY (2011)

Intern: $46,000
Non-intern: $34,600

FROM COLLEGE TO CAREER

Non-intern – 6.3 months
Intern – 2.5 months

AVERAGE RETENTION RATE

Interns:
1 Years – 76%
5 Years – 55%

Non-interns:
1 Years – 61%
5 Years – 44%

21

CHAPTER 2

IDENTIFYING WHAT YOU WANT

THE IMPORTANCE OF CULTURE IN DETERMINING WHAT YOU WANT

One of the most important things to talk about is how do you fit in. Why is that so important? All employees have essential human wants and needs despite the generation they were born into. These feelings, motivations, desires, and a sense of purpose actually matter. How people feel about coming to work, contributing, being able to be their authentic self, and feeling like they fit in, meaning they feel welcomed, and valued, is absolutely essential to employee engagement and to achieving business results.

This all ties back into a company achieving its organizational strategy. Organizations have to have the right employees with the right skills in the right place. Those employees want to know how and where they fit into the strategic direction. Employees need to know what their purpose is in coming to work every day. Employees need to understand how their contribution is helping the organization win. Now, both organizations and the people that work in them have needs. We need to talk about them openly and not reserved for closed-door office or conference room conversations.

There is power in having a shared sense of purpose. It does incredible things for people and groups trying to work together. Organizational strategy creates an immediate need and requires the aligning and developing of people to meet it if you hope to achieve that approach and be successful. Leaders of organizations should not shy away from

22

talking about the wants, needs, and motivations of employees. This type of conversation takes a level of transparency. For some leaders, it could be uncomfortable but, without that level of transparency, they can't build trust with you as an employee.

Being welcomed and valued is important and unique to each individual. That's why leaders and managers must get to know the people who work for them. Get to know who what they value, what they bring to the table even when that may feel different, new, or unfamiliar. Even when the people they're talking to don't automatically think the same way, or don't contribute in a way they're most comfortable with. Fitting in, knowing your purpose and feeling that you are both meeting your needs and those of the organization is good, but engagement and retention take more than that.

More than just fitting in, you want to feel valued. You want to feel welcomed. Not only when you come to work on a Monday or after a vacation. You want to feel that when they show up each day, people are genuinely happy to see you. Not from just a collegial standpoint, but that you're part of the organization. You want to feel like you matter and that your contributions help drives the execution of strategy.

Connecting with your leader doesn't have to be through an intensive check-in or meeting set on the calendar. Drive by sessions with your leader, just stopping by in the morning on the way to get coffee, or on your way in, can be just as empowering.

Another aspect of setting an environment to get the best business results is authenticity. Everyone wants to do their best and tap into their real potential, but people want to feel valued for who they are. You want to think that you're doing something good, something meaningful through your work, that the hours spent in the office matter; you're contributing to something greater than yourself. What enables this to happen is developing a sense of self-awareness. That taps into your feelings and heightens your sense of professional identity and gives you a greater feeling of self-worth.

Unfortunately, many organizations don't think about that unless it is pointed out. Here are a few things to be on the watch for in a company or organization to determine if being authentic is embraced or avoided. Do you see leaders, managers, and employees engaging each other across functions, across levels, and across generations? Is there friction or do things—for the most part—work fluidly?

Work is such a big part of our lives. Shouldn't we identify personally with our work and find satisfaction in what we do? Most everyone wants to be themselves. It's not easy trying to be someone or something you're not. It's stressful, and you spend all of that time in the office trying to fit into a mold that quite frankly was never really made for you. Organizations should understand that they need to appeal to the heart, the head and not just the wallet of their employees. Leaders of organizations need to have a level of consideration for the employee. They must create an environment where employees believe that it is good for them to work there, that they're being paid fairly and are valued and are helping the organization achieve business results.

CHAPTER 3

WORKING WITH A CO-OP ADVISOR THROUGH THE PROCESS

YOU OWN YOUR PLAN

You can't wait for an organization to see you as being a high potential or that you are an up-and-comer before you take advantage of doing things for your own career.

Most of us who are leaders in the workforce today grew up raised mainly by parents who were traditionalists or early Baby Boomers. And often, the counsel to us was to find a great company out of college, go there, work really hard, and apply yourself, make yourself indispensable, and you'll move up in the business. You will have a career path and a career plan, and you'll be on your way to making an excellent salary, having a retirement plan, and everything will take care of itself.

That's what we were told and what we were raised to think, but instead, we discovered a cruel irony.

Many of us watched our parents spend years in an organization— fifteen, twenty, twenty-five years—and end up being let go, laid off, downsized, outsized or right sized ... before the dream of a grand retirement, getting the gold watch, and monthly retirement checks in the mailbox came to fruition.

25

What we were told and believed just didn't happen. And I don't think it's ever going to come back again.

The reality is when you go into an organization, you're an 'at-will' employee, they know it, and you should know it. Many new employees don't realize they can be let go at any time for anything. That's what at-will means ... no loyalty to employees ... no good-faith between you and your employer. Your relationship with the company is purely transactional. As long as you fit into their plans or into the current economic conditions for the business—then you'll have a job. The minute something in that balance changes—you may find that you're out of a job.

This reality is why owning your own plan is essential.

You have to know what you want to do, who you want to be, where you want to go. The most important thing is when you go into any organization, you don't change your overall goal or dream of whom or what you want to become—those must be rock-solid objectives. You probably do or should view the organization as just a means to get you to where you want to go. At the earliest indication, the organization you are with no longer will help further you toward your goals—you should evaluate the situation and look for opportunities with other organizations to move your skills and capabilities to. What you do to move toward preparing yourself to reach your professional and career goals is your succession plan.

I think about what this has meant for my own career.

I had always thought that I wanted to be a senior executive in a Fortune 50 company. I had goals set that I believed would lead me to one of those positions. First and foremost, my goal was making vice president in a Fortune 50 company by the time I turned 40. I figured if I could make VP by 38 that would give me a good, solid 20 to 25 years in a company or in my profession at a high level. And then would subsequently retire with a substantial 401k and a lot of deferred compensation; young enough to enjoy a life away from the corporate grind. I had worked hard for many years to get to that place and made vice president at age 38.

But I got there and wondered, is this really what I want to do? I asked myself, what I am giving to get? One of the leaders—in a position I aspired to—said to me, *"the higher you go up, the more you give up."* That was an interesting observation, and it hit me hard. It was at that very moment when I realized I was living that reality: the higher I went, the more I had given up. And at that moment, I realized that I was giving up too much for too little in return.

Think about the impact of that simple truth.

This senior executive I spoke with talked about it openly. On his corporate climb, he'd given up time with his wife and his family to become the head of HR for a major organization. He had to make trades and sacrifices. And he had to ask for those to also be made by his family to enable him to get to that position.

I wondered, do I really want to do that?

Was it something I really felt so strongly about that I was willing to give up time that I would never get back with those most important to me for a job where I could easily be replaced? Was I willing to work hard making someone else rich, while at the same time making myself dependent on an organization? Did I want to live my life only on the weekends or with the permission of the company to have three weeks of my own life back each year as a gift called vacation ... where I would still be expected to be 'available' to the company. Hell no!

These decisions—answering these questions and addressing these considerations—is what you will be faced with, too.

I think it's important to get a complete perspective on this from someone who has lived and is reporting on what it is like to pursue the corporate dream of establishing a professional career as a high-level executive within a huge company.

Owning your succession plan is figuring out who you want to be and how to go after it—then making it happen.

There's a movie from a few years ago called *The Pursuit of Happyness* with Will Smith that has really stuck in my mind. In the film, Will Smith portrays Chris Gardner. Gardner had invested heavily in a device known as a Bone Density Scanner. He feels he'll 'have it made' selling these devices. However, since they are only marginally better than the current technology, but at a much higher price, they do not sell. As Gardner tries to figure out how what to do, his wife leaves him; he loses his house, empties his bank account and maxes out his credit cards. Losing it all, forced to live on the street with his son, Gardner is now desperate to find a steady job. The most fascinating scene of the movie to me is when he is walking down the street (presumably the Wall Street area of New York). He has had a hard day trying to sell the Bone Density Scanners to doctors' offices and hospitals to make money to feed his son. As he walks, he sees a well-dressed man getting out of a red Ferrari in front of a building. Will Smith smiles, and says to the guy "I just have two questions for you: What do you do, and how do you do it?" He is amazed to learn that the guy was a stockbroker. Even more amazing to him is that in a quick conversation, he discovers that you don't need to go to college to become a stockbroker ... you just need to be good with numbers and good with people. After the guy exchanges a couple of quick words and a joke with Gardner, he enters the building. As Gardner looks around, he notices how happy everyone seems, how everyone coming and going was smiling. It is the moment that he begins his pursuit of 'happyness' and decides to become a stockbroker.

When I saw that scene and reflected on it, I thought it profound and prophetic.

I saw it as something anybody could do for their career (and for their life as well). All you have to do when you see somebody doing what you want to do, or that has what you want—whether it's the right car, the right job, the right house, whatever it is, but having the life you want for yourself—is have the courage and the conviction to ask them, *"Excuse me, can you tell me what you do and how I could do that for myself?"* You won't come across to them as odd. I've experienced that most successful people, those who believe like I do in paying it forward will answer you. They're not going to item-by-item tell you how to conduct your own life or live it, but they'll tell you what they did. And then you can take that and fashion it into a plan for how you can then go after this in your own life.

That is what I have done.

I sought out people who were in the role I aspired to, I asked them for their resume, I studied their experiences and what they had done. Almost all of them were very young for the position. They had a meteoric rise through the ranks of not just one organization but others as well. And they took risks by moving from company to company, from state to state, from location to location; some took international assignments. All of them had a theme of continued progress and moving forward. And they had all networked hard by making connections with other people in their field. They worked smart to meet people who are in the roles they one day wanted to have for themselves—their targeted next level in their professional career.

I studied them; looked at what they'd done to get to where they were, and I thought about it. How can I put myself in beneficial situations where:

(A) I could network,

(B) I could meet people,

(C) I could learn to speak industry language and

(D) I could speak industry language with industry professionals.

If there were online magazines I should read, I would subscribe to them. If there were books that I should be reading, I bought them and started voraciously reading them. I started looking at where and what time these people would congregate. Was there a society they belonged to? Was there a set meeting place and time? Was it 6:30pm on a Tuesday night? Whatever that was, I decided to be there. If there were a conference they all went to once a year, I would be sure to go to that conference.

I boosted my LinkedIn profile where people can see me, see who I am, look at my background. People reach out to me now all the time to network with me or introduce themselves through LinkedIn. Granted, I am very selective about who I connect with or rather connect with on LinkedIn because my brand is important to me. All 1,600-some odd people in my LinkedIn network are those I have either worked with in the past or plan to work with in some capacity in the future. I do not add people to my network just because their background seems cool. That's just not how I work. Through intention, each of my contacts has to be a good connection who would represent me well (as I hope that I do for them).

The job you want is out there—you just might not be ready for it.

It can be hard to not get frustrated and throw your resume out there thinking, "*I hope to hell somebody will give me a shot even though I know I am not 100% what they need.*"

Don't do that.

I spent ten years working at and figuring out how to optimize my approach and myself for the job market targeting an eventual climb to the executive levels in a large company.

As I have shared, many people don't realize your resume only gets you the interview.

The interview gets you the job.

It's not good enough to have a great resume if you can't sell yourself. You have to be able to sell yourself as the embodiment of the resume.

Remember what I said earlier about preparation?

Everything I just shared with you—all the preceding in this chapter—is just that. It is what you need to do to prepare for co-op opportunities, and full-time employment and that preparation is what you should expect to be told when working with your advisor. If not, you have at least heard it here from me.

Next up—in the following chapters—you'll read real stories from current college students, and recent graduates internship and co-op experiences. They are grouped into different disciplines and roles. Their words are raw, real, and relevant and obtained by interview and have only been lightly edited and revised to preserve interviewee anonymity. What you will read next is the 'how to' get the most out of your college co-op and internship program experience ... as your first step toward the corner office.

CHAPTER 4

FINANCE & ACCOUNTING

Despite job cuts in banking and financial services during the recession, the future is positive, with finance and accountancy leading the way in the sector's recovery. You could work in areas, including insurance, financial planning, investments and pensions, accountancy and finance, and banking.

WHAT DO EMPLOYERS LOOK FOR?

While there are opportunities for graduates from a range of subjects, requirements set by smaller companies may vary. Employers in this sector place great emphasis on work experience. Many firms offer internships, summer placements or a year in industry for undergraduate students, which may lead to permanent jobs or entry onto graduate schemes. Visit individual company websites or your university careers service for the latest work placements and internships.

Employers generally require candidates with a real interest in finance; analytical skills; attention to detail and accuracy; and the capacity to work with figures and statistics.

HOW DO I FIND A JOB?

Many graduates begin their career by being accepted into a company's entry-level career position. You'll usually follow a structured training program and have the opportunity to work in various departments within the company before selecting your preferred area. When it comes to the leading employers, there are the 'big four' accountancy and financial services firms: Deloitte; Ernst & Young; KPMG; and PwC. However, there are also many small and medium-sized enterprises (SMEs), and this type of employer provides excellent career prospects for graduates. However, recruitment, selection, and training arrangements may not be as formal. Entry-level in accountancy also exist within charities and not-for-profit organizations, but the majority of finance opportunities are with profit-generating businesses.

WHAT'S THE WORKING CULTURE?

Graduates can expect:

- employee benefits, such as pension plans, private healthcare, joining bonuses and sports club membership;
- good opportunities for progression;
- starting salaries of between $45,000 and $60,000;
- substantial bonuses in some finance professions;
- to work long hours in a fast-paced office environment.

CO-OP PARTICIPANT INTERVIEWS

Interviewee #1 of 4

I started college with very, very vague ideas of what I wanted to do with my life. I chose my major (business) and my concentration (accounting and management) almost at random, picking the subject I enjoyed most in high school, noting that it was just the kind of systematic analysis that I loved to do. This confusion was not cleared up by the time I had to choose my first co-op almost a year-and-a-half later. I had only the slightest clues about what career paths were available for someone with my interests, and those clues mainly revolved around doing taxes. My family wasn't much help, as most of them considered their dream job to be one that didn't involve math. Luckily my university is known for experiential learning, so there was a vast resource of knowledgeable advisors, professors, and upperclassmen at my disposal, but still—it was stressful!

The firm I worked at was a firm that I met at a career fair at on campus, one I probably would have avoided if there wasn't a class assignment connected to it. I gave them my resume, did an interview, was offered a job on the spot, and accepted—even though it was the exact opposite of what I was looking for. The job description wasn't appealing, and it was in the city when I had been hoping for a move to New York, but I liked the people I spoke to, and I liked the feel of the office (and I loved that they wanted me enough to make an immediate offer). I listened to my advisor, knowing that this experience could be the springboard I needed to jump into other career paths that interested me more later on.

The firm is a large regional CPA firm in New England. They have just about 250 employees spread across four offices in three states. They were dedicated to providing "the highest quality accounting, tax, and advisory services" to a wide range of clients across a broad variety of industries. The company boasts their core values of being client focused, maintaining the highest level of integrity, hiring a knowledgeable team of industry specialists, and supporting an entrepreneurial spirit within the work environment. It is a company that has consistently been named one of the best places to work, and after working there for six months, I can see why. Going to work was always fun. People worked hard, as accountants so often do. But they understood the importance of a work-life balance. There were usually office-wide events - celebrations for everything from birthdays to the end of a tax season, to the start of baseball season.

Schedules were flexible, there were often baked goods in the kitchen, and ties could be left at the door.

The firm and my university go way back regarding the co-op program. The company had a relationship with our advisors on par with those of the Big 4, even though it was only a regional firm. That involvement and the commitment the company had to their co-ops made it the perfect place to start my professional career. They had a formal training program that provided the essential foundation we would need to complete any of the work thrown at us. The training was continuous, and we often spent our Saturday mornings in a conference room, catching up with each other in between reviewing how to report a sale of home and how to allocate management fees. We had a senior manager and a supervisor who led the training, as well as multiple others who were never too busy to answer our questions. But even though we had that help, we were never treated as interns. In their eyes, we were entry-level employees, seasonal workers who would lessen the burden of another busy season.

Employees generally fell into two categories at the firm: tax or audit. There were other smaller, subdivisions but odds are, you were either one or the other. The co-ops mostly made up the bottom tier of the tax department. Above the interns, you had the associates, supervisors, managers, senior executives, principals, and partners. Our direct contacts were often supervisors, but even as an entry-level employee, you had contact with people at every level. For example, the bulk of my work came from a supervisor, but a sizeable chunk came from the principal in the corner office.

The co-ops were hired to help the tax team prepare returns in the months before April 15th. In my role as a preparer, I would be one of the first to go through the client documents, organize them, filter out what isn't needed, scan them in if necessary, and then prepare the return. When complete, it would go up to at least one reviewer, before being signed off by a partner. Seeing as we were the first step in the process, we often set the tone for how quickly and efficiently the process would be completed. Though the work could get monotonous and repetitive, it was easy to see the impact our efforts had on the company, keeping it fulfilling. It helped that we were never treated as interns. We weren't fetching coffee, and in return, we were expected to act like adults. We needed to be self-sufficient and proactive—reaching out when we had a problem, professionally conducting ourselves, and managing our own time and responsibilities.

My primary responsibility was preparing 1040s and 1041s as they were given to me. Though most people would give work directly to a particular co-op, there was a pool of simple returns that we could go to when looking for something to do. Once we had a return on our to-do list, I would go through the source documents, weeding out any unnecessary information, inputting the rest of it into the company tax software, and then sending the return and any outstanding points to the responsible person for review. The supervisor I mainly worked with also liked having me input the information into an Excel template to make reviewing easier. Depending on whom I was working with, the return might come back with notes and errors that needed to be fixed. We were also tasked with preparing extensions for the incomplete returns. In the post-4/15 slump that accountants always face, the co-ops worked on an entry-level manual that featured instructions and tips for common issues.

One of the hardest parts of my job was the lack of variety in my days. I was hired for one specific reason—to prepare tax returns—and I almost never got to branch out. I was given a fair amount of responsibility, and I enjoyed the work, but it didn't give me many line items to put on my resume. Luckily 1040's and 1041's are so complex and differ so wildly based on the individual the work didn't get jump-out-a-window boring. But I wish that I had gained more exposure to the other pieces of tax accounting. I got minimal exposure to foreign tax rules and did only the simplest parts of a corporate return. I never got to sit in on a client meeting or an idea pitch.

That's not to say I didn't learn anything, though. The firm had a top-notch training program. The first two weeks of the co-op were spent in a conference room, being taught what a W-2 is and who files a 1040 versus a 1041. The higher-ups assumed we were coming in with zero tax experience. That training provided the foundation for nearly every project I needed to complete. At that point in my academic career, I had only taken two basic accounting classes that provided me with a beginner's knowledge of debits and credits and balance sheets (oh my!). Though walking into the job without any developed accounting skills was intimidating, it was never a problem. Most of the struggles we faced were due to inexperience with the software, rather than a lack of tax expertise.

I was highly dependent on my computer and the internet. We used internet-based software to prepare our tax returns, another website tracked the status and preparation of each of the returns, yet another software held electronic copies of every source document and return received pretty much since the company's inception. I had never used software like this so heavily in my life. Forgetting about all the technical aspects of accounting this job taught me, this software taught me how to troubleshoot to solve a problem. However, having this technology at my fingertips definitely minimized my understanding of the final return (can you say Millennial issues?). Because the computer would generate the form based on my inputs and selections, I never actually learned where exactly these numbers went across the schedules. I just knew that if you input that number onto that screen, it would show up somewhere on the form.

It truly does take a village to submit a tax return. The responsible person was the person 'in charge' of that particular return. They would contact the client and collect the source documents. They would then give the return to either an associate or co-op for preparation. While preparing the return, we used anyone available to help. Another co-op might be able to help, the unlucky associate sitting at their desk when you went searching might be able to help, or you might need to go back to the source and ask the RP. After preparation, the return goes back to the responsible people who will either send it off for review or look through it themselves. The co-op's goal (and unofficial job description) was to make life easier for the person directly above us. Whether that was listing out the missing source documents or making the PDF's a uniform orientation, we were tasked with doing anything in our power to save the person above us a little time and frustration.

Looking back on co-op I realize how lucky I was to get the training that I did. The year-and-a-half before this internship was filled with a lot of massive lecture halls, basic intro lessons, and classes not related to my major at all. Sure, the two accounting classes I had taken were useful in providing background, but it wasn't essential. The econ classes had no part in my job, except perhaps making it possible for me to follow a discussion on whether a flat tax could ever come about. Supply chain was just an 11-letter word, Shakespeare or Chaucer never even came up in conversation, and no one ever asked my opinion on fracking. The most necessary skills were the soft skills like organization, punctuality, presentation, and time management, which I've learned over the course of my time in school. The one course that does come to mind though was a class I took my first semester, Experiential Entrepreneurship. The entire basis of this class was to create an original business plan with a group of your peers. There were presentations throughout the semester and a speaker series connected to the class. Unfortunately, I had what might have been the worst group in group project history, but still, I loved this class, and I credit it with teaching me my air of professionalism. The odd thing is I absolutely did not conduct myself professionally while in this class. I was so desperate to give the best project despite the lack of support that I became an intense micromanager who became flustered during presentations. So, what's the connection? I think of everything I wish I had done during that class and present myself in that manner. Ever since, whenever I feel myself getting too intense or too argumentative, I am able to rein it in, wishing to avoid the future embarrassment. It's weird, I know, but it seems to be working.

A wise professor once pointed out you can't grow without feedback, and though the firm sometimes forgot about that, the final evaluation was detailed enough. The final assessment was a standard form from my university that I went over with my boss on my last day. He made comments on my organization skills, time management skills, and technical growth. But he made critiques as well, pointing out things that I needed to learn to reach the highest level of success. He told me I was quiet and that people would often forget about me. He said that I needed to be more assertive and better about asking people for work when things got slow. Because I remained in the background, people didn't always know what I could do, and I would, therefore, miss out on some bigger opportunities.

Hearing this feedback was invaluable, especially the positive. My senior year of high school I received a severe concussion playing soccer that had some lasting effects. After a rapidly deteriorating memory and a vocabulary that was seemingly slashed in half caused me to struggle in all my classes freshman year of college, I was diagnosed with a minor learning disability that summer. My executive function was suddenly dysfunctional—I had developed a facet of ADHD that affects the working memory. I found that I could not learn in a classroom setting anymore. It was boring, and my mind wandered, I was always a step or two (or five) behind everyone else, and I wouldn't really understand the topic until I was able to work through the homework on my own time. This made participating in class very difficult, and my new mortal enemy was any teacher that cold-called. I was terrified to go on co-op and learn that all those 'normal' college kids with their 'healthy' brains really were better than me. And though everyone but me thought I was overreacting, it was still nice to hear that I "would do very well in [the accounting] industry." Everyone needs that validation that they are on the right path and I suddenly felt like I could breathe again. And even the critiques my boss had for me had nothing to do with how unintelligent I was, buoying me up further.

Hearing that feedback and talking to the many different people at the firm illuminated my future path much further than the previous six months. Though I didn't make any drastic changes, I did extend my program to five years and tacked on a master's in Accounting that I would complete during my fifth year (and also decided I'd sit for my CPA). Stepping out into the real world made me realize just how many things you could do with an accounting degree, and I was anxious to try them all on for size before graduating. Just hearing about the experiences of all these established adults and listening to them debate the merits of an MSA versus an MST made me understand what might work for me and what I could definitely never do. Unfortunately, the changes I made were about all I had control over, short of changing my major, as the university curriculum is so rigid, but I do have a multitude of ideas of what to do for my next co-op and beyond.

Overall, I couldn't be happier with my entry into the business world. Of all the professional experience on my resume, working for the firm definitely ranks toward the top. The funny thing is I anticipated hating it. I thought I'd be bored out of my mind, resentful of how much free time it ate up and the professional façade the job would invariably require. I had a near breakdown before starting because of their comprehensive beard policy, totally ignoring the fact that I can't grow a beard! Luckily, I was 100% wrong. The environment, though professional, was informal and young. People wanted to talk to you, not just work with you.

We were kept very busy, working a fair amount of overtime, but you had plenty of other co-ops to lean on and great advisors to help you out. I came out of that co-op feeling as if I had a better idea of what I wanted out of a career and also knowing that there would be people to reach out to if I were to ever need anything. All these praises being sung; however, I chose not to return to the firm for my second co-op. Though I was overall pleased, the company did handle a couple of situations in a way that I did not agree with, leaving a bad taste in my mouth at the time. The company hired too many co-ops during my cycle, causing us to have a lot of downtime both early and late in my six-month stint. Also, our boss worked in an office 20 minutes away from where half of us were. Even with phone, IM, and email, it was easy to feel abandoned. It didn't help that the interns' cubicles in the city office were quite separate from everyone else, which was a constant reminder that we were 'different.' I don't fault them for creating this atmosphere, as we were the first crop of co-ops to work in the brand-new city office and everyone was still figuring things out, but I hope it's an area they concentrate on fixing.

All in all, I can't imagine going to a 'normal' school. The fact that my university gives us a trial run of the real world is the most invaluable educational experience I have had. It not only allows you to see if you are on the right, but you can also rub elbows with people who have been there and done that, hearing their experiences first-hand. It helps students (like me) who struggle in classrooms and who always question if they have what it takes to make it in their industry of choice. Experiential learning makes us employable, it makes us ready for the future, and it makes us excited to see what's to come.

Interviewee #2 of 4

My co-op was spent at the organization working in Wealth Management. The co-op lasted seven months. As a finance student, I was particularly interested in learning about the investment management aspect of Wealth Management. The team I worked for specifically, provided services such a bill payment and charitable donation services for clients, but those fields were secondary to my initial interest. I felt wealth management is also one of the rare areas in finance where you get to interact with clients on a personal level, which further peaked my interest.

I provided value to the company (or the team) by doing project-based work with my financial knowledge or 'expertise' at a relatively low cost. I also helped bring new ideas to the table that my managers appeared to appreciate, as they were often implemented. The group hired co-ops for three main reasons, in my opinion. Firstly, the projects I would work on would often be too project related for them to devote one of their assistants to since they often were busy with day-to-day tasks. Having a co-op allowed my managers to delegate projects that would take a long time without compromising the time and availability of other team members. Secondly, one of the financial advisors on the team attended my university, and it was very evident that he received satisfaction from having a co-op and being part of my university community. Finally, co-ops provide labor and manpower to an office at a relatively low price. My managers had an equity stake in the group, and I think (nobody explicitly said this) that hiring a co-op instead of an additional full-time employee allowed them to retain more earnings.

The organization's mission statement spoke to the importance of putting client relationships first and is proud to conduct our business based on five unwavering principles: client focus, respect for the individual, teamwork, responsible citizenship, and integrity." At organization, as a part of the team, it was very evident that the financial advisors and team members cared for their clients on a personal level and thoroughly enjoyed working with them.

The organization has over 15,000 employees. However, it did not have an overly corporate feel. Since our team was quite small, it had a very entrepreneurial spirit and small-team environment where you felt like you knew everyone on an individual level. The organization is broken up into various teams that manage their own clients and primarily operate their unit as a business entity separate from the organization. The co-op commitment is on an individual, or group level, rather than a corporate initiative. In the local office, I was the only co-op, but I know that other organization locations also have co-op interns.

My position was quite closed off from the rest of the organization, and I was essentially a local group employee rather than an employee of the organization. There was little interaction on a professional level with the remainder of the organization (personally, everyone was very nice and approachable). Within my team, I was often the point person for whenever a team member had a project or idea that would take several days or weeks until implemented, as well as helping with administrative tasks when I had downtime.

The wealth management industry was undergoing extreme changes during the time I worked with the organization. New regulations were set to completely change the compensation structure for financial advisors, and new fiduciary standards were changing the wealth management landscape. One of my projects was helping ensure all client accounts in the organization system had adapted to new regulatory requirements. Additionally, the high return of the S&P in past years has clients second-guessing management fees and active management, and leaning more toward passive investment management that tracks the S&P500 and therefore avoids charges. For my team, their value-added consisted of going beyond investment management and more into goals-based planning and acting as peace-of-mind for their clients. Another challenge for the financial advisors was tracking their prospects and leads, with which I helped implement a new process using Salesforce.

My day-to-day duties changed based off what my manager's needed help with. On a weekly basis, I had the responsibility of preparing a performance report, which outlined assets and liabilities of the team, incoming and outgoing assets, and a small report tracking the financial advisor's effectiveness in converting leads/prospects into clients. Another task that occurred almost daily but was subject to change was researching prospects, attempting to create a picture around their net worth, social interests and personal life (age/family/marital status).

The majority of the duties I took on that went beyond the job description happened when I had little to do and could tell that the rest of the team was busy. This would range from helping a financial advisor calculate a client's portfolio return on a basis different than the standard the organization platform, to offering to get lunch or coffee for the team in preparation for an important meeting.

My role was highly collaborative; so much so that I cannot recall a project I was assigned that did not include working with team members. Often the collaboration would entail me receiving instructions from a manager, then doing the work or returning with a question for clarity. Furthermore, we often held small meetings where we would action plan a project. An example of this what helping one of the financial advisors expand their LinkedIn presence, to help increase his networking capabilities and online presence.

The technical functions of my position required strong Excel skills, a simple understanding of Salesforce and a willingness to learn the organization's platform that is difficult at first but powerful once understood.

I would say that my co-op required entry-level finance courses (financial management and investments) to help understand investing basics, the time value of money, and scenario analysis (for example, using Monte Carlo simulations).

The key goal of any of my projects was to expand the Wealth Management practice regarding assets under management and 'performance credits' produced by the financial advisors.

Key data I generated on a regular basis were the aforementioned performance reports of the team. For this, I used Excel in coordination with the organization platform, as well as PowerPoint to present the data.

During my time at the organization, I operated a PC and a Bloomberg Terminal (Bloomberg was used on rare occasions).

The co-op specifically involved familiarizing myself with the organization Wealth Management platform, which was not possible before joining the organization and had to be done on the job.

In coordination with my managers, I helped with the co-op interviews for the next semester. From a presentation standpoint, I would use PowerPoint for various tasks, such as the performance reports or when I would present ideas that I thought could help make the practice run more efficiently. An example of this was a presentation to show the financial advisors how to more effectively use Salesforce.

I was not given a written evaluation, but was offered a position for the fall and moving forward. It was evident to me that the team thoroughly enjoyed working with me, and on a personal level has kept in contact with me since my co-op. Even after I turned down their offer, they repeatedly asked me to reconsider staying onboard into the spring semester.

Working at the organization helped me become a more effective team player, and improved my understanding of how to balance collaboration with different personalities. It also increased my ability to identify issues in the workplace and work on methods of problem-solving. The role also instilled in me a greater understanding of personal finance, building wealth and responsible investing.

One of the managers and alums of my university on the team recommend a particular professor for my Working Capital course, so I followed his recommendation. Other than that, I would not say that the experience impacted my course selection. However, it did give me a breadth of knowledge to carry into my Portfolio Management class. The most applicable course to Wealth Management was investments, and even though I took this class after the co-op, Portfolio Management was highly relevant as well. The principles that helped with the co-op were an understanding of time value of money, the role that expenses play in long-term investing, fundamental investing ideas (passive versus active, active beta, ETFs versus Mutual Funds), and Monte Carlo simulations.

My on-the-job experience gave me a much clearer picture of the sales aspect of Wealth Management. In class, we merely learn about the financial principles of the industry but do not consider how the ability to sell yourself and your team ultimately decides the success of a financial advisor.

I would consider the role as adequate in making use of my skills. I feel I could have contributed or been stimulated much more on the investments side during my time at the organization. The lack of involvement or inclusion in investing decisions (not that I expect to contribute, but it would have been interesting to sit in during the process) is perhaps the only regret of my experience.

I enjoyed the co-op and would recommend it to other students seriously considering a career in Wealth Management. Personally, I am pleased with my increased understanding of retirement saving and personal finance, and even though I do not plan to pursue a career as a financial advisor, my personal development at the organization made the experience valuable.

The co-op could be improved by including more investment-oriented activities or learning opportunities. Ultimately, these are the interest-drivers for students going into wealth management, and I feel that more exposure to the investment process itself would have created more interest in the role from a personal standpoint.

Interviewee #3 of 4

I currently work as a commercial real estate co-op at an international firm. The firm is a global commercial real estate services organization that operates in approximately 68 countries. The local office is composed of capital markets, downtown brokerage, suburban brokerage, retail services, and other support for the brokers. On the research team, I work closely with the Director of Research to provide support to all channels of the business by updating the internal database, creating a new system of presenting marketing intelligence, providing customized research, and other ad-hoc inquiries. I am in my fifth month at this position; my position will come to a close at the end of this month (total work time of 5 ½ months). As a 3rd year student pursuing a combined degree in Economics and Business Administration with a concentration in finance, I was attracted to this co-op position because of the way it integrates economics and business. In my day-to-day, I am able to use the analytical and problem-solving skills that I have obtained through finance course as well as the theoretical and cause-and-effect skills that I have gained from economics courses.

The co-op program has been a longstanding role at the company. However, my boss, the Director of Research, started working at here a year ago, so I, along with another co-op, are his 2nd and 3rd co-ops. The original co-op position was created to support the research team in performing quarterly database updates as well as daily and long-term ad-hoc projects. Since my boss was hired, he saw the co-op program as an opportunity to enhance our experience as co-ops and holistically introduce us to all aspects of the real estate sector of business as well as use our new perspectives and skills to do more with the data. With the former, my boss took the initiative and hired two co-ops this cycle; with the intention that we would be able to find opportunities in the data we have and also be able to research our own personal projects.

The company as a company is focused on their enterprising culture, which allows professionals to think differently, sharing great ideas and creating practical solutions that help clients accelerate their success. The company encourages its employees to embody a creative and entrepreneurial spirit at work, allowing employees to be passionate and take responsibility for their work. From my experience at the company, I believe the company's focus on enterprising culture to be accurate. Although there are different cultures, or 'vibes,' between the team I work on (research) and the primary focus of the employer (brokers), we both have opportunities to be independent and entrepreneurial in our work. From my personal experience, I have the chance to do my own research, by looking at data and producing projects from it based on aspects I find interesting.

The organization has 400+ offices worldwide. In the office where I worked, I would estimate there are 100 people composed of the brokerage team, investment services, research, marketing, graphics, IT, HR, etc. The company has a relatively small co-op program with only myself and one other co-op (compared to my last co-op assignment where 50 co-ops started the same time as I did.) The co-op program has existed at the company for several years. My current boss has been working at the company for less than a year and is invested in the co-op program, already expanding the number of co-ops from 1 to 2 in my cycle. At my previous co-op, there was a stronger and more established co-op program (shadow initiatives, opportunities to meet fellow co-ops, one-on-one sessions with company co-op coordinator, etc.) primarily due to the size of the enterprise.

However, I do not feel that I am missing out on the benefits I received at my prior co-op. Being on a smaller team allows me to be able to take on more responsibility and work with different departments. And my boss' commitment to the co-op program and making sure we have a holistic experience in real estate has proven to be an unmatchable experience.

Like any other real estate company, the workhorses of the organization are the brokers. Our team supports the organization by answering any and all requests from the brokers, and other teams, to support the daily functions of the organization. I like to think we provide the foundation for the company. Every quarter the research team publishes a market overview that summarizes the current market conditions and forecasts possible future conditions. Without this information, and information like it, brokers would not be able to go about their daily functions as efficiently and productively. Brokers would not be able to sell a building, without knowing the current rent and vacancy trends and what they're forecasted to be in the future, information that my team provides.

One problem that existed before I came to the company was the company as a whole was striving to be more innovative and diverse. My first week at the job, the company was preparing for their annual seminar and annual showcase and forum of real estate from internal professionals, and I had the chance to shadow preparation for one of the panels for the event. A couple of the associates relayed to me how this year they made it a point to have a more diverse panel, that included younger associates from a broader range of specialties. Also, there was a push to find a way to present marketing intelligence in a new and innovative way, a task that I was quickly charged with to brainstorm and execute ideas. Other goals were to update the weak internal database, we approached this by working extensively in the database, reclassifying buildings to decrease the margin of error that our reports used to have. Another challenge was reaching contacts at different organizations. I approached this problem by using external resources to find out contact information and working with marketing to organize this data in a format that is fast and easy to use.

The position I held consisted of a consistent quarterly project, ad-hoc week/bi-weekly projects and daily data pulls and quick research requests. A typical day not near quarter end includes working on a long-term, weekly project as well as dealing with a handful of daily requests. A typical day near quarter end revolves around doing vacancy reports and ensuring our database is updated for our market overview. For example, a day could start with working with IT to pull queries on a specific type of building or submarket were looking into. Then using that data to build pivot tables and charts for an upcoming sales pitch. Then pulling different market reports for brokers as requests come in. And perhaps once the tables are created for the presentation, looking at the data again from my perspective and seeing if there are any potential personal projects and research that could stem from it. Other projects include pulling aerials on a site, tenant tracking, looking up zonal codes, keeping up with real estate in the media, researching a new trend in the market, and many other things.

As I mentioned before, this position had a handful of opportunities to do personal research. I would view these projects as beyond the standard job description because I was looking into different things that I was particularly interested in and related the searches to data, opposed to being assigned a task. Also, I believe that I am more creative than the counterparts on my team and have skills formatting slides and data into a visually appealing presentation, so I took the lead in helping the marketing team and assisting the research team regarding visual aid. Additionally, I had the opportunity to sit in as a representative of the company at a few speaker series as well as cross-company real estate meetings. In these roles, I made sure I recorded accurate and pertinent information and reported back the findings to my superiors.

A majority of the work I do in this position is both collaborative and independent work done within the research team that then goes on to support other channels of the business. The research team works most closely with the graphics and marketing team to provide a product that has been well researched as well as visually appealing to the end user. For the most part, the other co-op and I split up projects as they come in based on our current load and interests. After we finish our work, our boss (the Director of Research) usually checks over the work and gives us critique and ways to improve the work before we send it off to whoever requested it.

This position requires me to be proficient in Microsoft Office applications; I use Excel, Word, and PowerPoint every day. Additionally, I use internal and external databases to pull information on buildings, sales, leases, tenants, etc. Basic GIS mapping is used. However, most of our larger GIS projects are outsourced.

My academic background definitely helped me perform in this position efficiently. My educational background allows me to be familiar with financial reports, specifically a company's 10k, earnings calls, balance sheets, income statements, etc. as well as be able to interpret the figures and numbers in these reports. For example, analyzing the financial state of a company and the likelihood of a company to start a new capital project by looking at debt-equity ratios. Other financial tools that I learned in an academic setting that are helpful in the position are loan payment schedules, debt, and the present value of money.

Additionally, knowing how to create and interpret graphs and charts while recognizing outliers and margins of errors have been extremely helpful. Knowledge gained from economics courses are also valuable tools, knowing how different exogenous factors affect supply and demand and how that relates to different markets, specifically real estate.

The overarching goal of the research team is to provide clients, brokers, and any other person who has a request for the most accurate and relevant data in a visually appealing way for them to successfully secure a deal, land a client, sell a property, etc. Another general goal of our team and the company as a whole is keeping up with the entrepreneurial goals that company pushes as a whole, staying innovative and asking questions. For example, as I explain in other questions, the roadshow and updating the internal database overall were tools to make the company more creative and make our research more accurate for our end users.

I mostly worked with internal and external databases. Also, I used Excel v-lookups, weighted averages, pivot tables, charts, graphs, filters, conditional formatting, etc.

One major project that I worked on during the position was a project called 'The Roadshow.' Before coming to the company, the way they presented market intelligence done the same way every time and were very outdated. My boss charged me and my fellow co-op to come up with a new way to present the market intelligence, one that had both new ways to present data and that was visually appealing. In this project, I analyzed the data in our internal database and created customized charts and graphs that are refreshable from quarter to quarter. We worked very closely with the marketing team to make a presentation that was both visually appealing and up to date on technology, most notably having a landing page and multiple ways to navigate the presentation. After the data end of the roadshow was completed, we worked with our boss to interpret the data and understand what the charts were saying about the market. The information then went on to support the published Quarterly Market Report.

To get this co-op position, I had to participate in the interview process. Before talking in person, I had to submit my resume as well as have an informational phone interview to learn more about the company and the position. During the in-person interview, I was asked about my previous co-op and work experience, courses that I took relevant to the job position, familiarity with different technical tools, and overall interest in real estate and the company. Post accepting the offer, I had to submit tax forms.

Because I have not completed this co-op position, I have not received a written evaluation of my performance as of yet. I have had conversations with my boss about performance, and they have all been positive, but not constructive.

Coming to my university, I really wanted to use the co-op program to test out different sectors of the business field to determine which was most compatible with my skills and interests. In my last co-op I explored the retail sector of business, and now I am currently studying the real estate sector. This position succeeded in allowing me to understand and explore a different area of business, and I am truly grateful. Additionally, this position allowed me to see the intersection of my two majors in full force. I would say this work experience aided my career development by enhancing my skills and knowledge in real estate as well as learning soft skills that are crucial in navigating the business world today.

After being in this position, I'm leaning toward taking Real Estate Finance as one of my finance concentration electives. I think if I took this class before this co-op I would have been able to tackle a more complex project that came along, and would also be able to understand the brokers and experts better. Although required, taking Investments in the future will also build on the information and skills learned in this position. Additionally, in my future economics courses, I'll be able to consider different things learned with a newfound real estate lens.

The courses that were most applicable to my co-op were Financial Management, Financial Accounting, Intro to Computer Science, Intro to Macroeconomics, Intro to Microeconomics, Macroeconomic Theory, Microeconomic Theory, Statistics, and Organizational Behavior. Financial Management taught me about debt vs. equity models and how funding is related to purchasing a building, capital budgeting, as well as taught me about loan payment schedules and the present value of money. Financial Accounting introduced me to financial statements like balance sheets and income statements. In Computer Science, I learned about navigating Excel and Access, and I currently use Excel daily, building pivot tables and charts and coding equations. The economics courses I've taken have taught me how different exogenous factors affect supply and demand and how that relates to different markets, specifically real estate. Economics has also taught me about looking at various models and determining factors to help forecast the market. Statistics helped with interpreting graphs and charts and identifying outliers and margins of error. Because I took Organizational Behavior before this co-op position, I am more cognizant of different roles of the company, different types of leadership, HR tools, and I am more actively aware of diversity (which I personally feel the company lacked in). Although Organizational Behavior didn't give me the technical skills needed to perform in this role, the course definitely helped me realize why people do what they do and observe different situations through a more professional lens.

The course also helped with relationship management, identifying that different people have different leadership and working styles and adjusting the way I navigate situations to produce the best end result. The courses that were least applicable to my co-op were Marketing, International Business, Business Calculus, and Entrepreneurship.

In my on-the-job experience, I have more sense of accountability, my boss did not check everything I did, and sometimes I have to think on my feet and act quickly. Whereas in an academic setting, I feel like it is a slower paced environment, I am able to review things multiple times, and if I get something wrong, it has no real-life impact. I have never taken a real estate class, so in this co-op position there are a lot of conversations and topics that are new to me, and I have to interpret them differently. In class, I learn information to pass a test and/or receive a good grade in the class. I learn what I need to get by and don't commit everything to memory. Whereas in a work setting, I have to learn information and commit it to memory, building on knowledge every day and using information determined to contribute to larger projects.

I felt technically prepared for this position and was confident using the databases and Microsoft Office applications. However, I don't believe my technical skills were as challenged as it could have been and I did not learn that many new skills in this regard.

Overall, I was satisfied with the co-op; I received a holistic view of real estate and got to combine my financial skills and economic interest to work on some interesting projects. However, some of the work was repetitive and elementary, so that was the one downside. I also don't see a lot of room for growth on the team I'm in. A factor that would probably stop me from returning in the future. I would recommend this position to someone doing a first-time co-op and someone who is interested in real estate, economics, and finance. I would recommend the job two opposite types of people, someone who is highly interested in data and can sit with it to find new information and be satisfied with doing this work repeatedly. The other type of person who I would recommend this position to is someone who has a high self-initiative to ask other departments for atypical work on top of their day-to-day work.

One aspect that I didn't like about this co-op was the fact that I didn't get to present the projects I worked on. To improve the position for others, I would suggest my boss allow the co-ops to give information they worked on, even if it was on a smaller scale, to test the co-ops knowledge and practice presentation skills. Also, I think the position would be enhanced with more hands-on experience, shadowing other teams, and having one-on-ones with members of each team, aspects that come with a more structured co-op program, much like my last co-op. I would also suggest a more formal training period.

Interviewee #4 of 4

I worked in the Finance Department at a pharmaceutical company. I was specifically in the procurement expertise area where I worked as a buyer for the company. As a co-op, I was placed in the Lab Supplies buying unit which means I and the other co-op were responsible for ordering all the items and services classified as a lab supply which included everything from reagents in life sciences to beakers to human serum to run analysis on. Services included things such as lab equipment repair and scientist consultations for assistance on tests and analysis. I would approve requisitions (requests) for the product in one system then create that same request in another system to get approved by the appropriate members of the business who were working on the project or needed the items. From there, I would create Purchase Orders that would be sent to vendors and used to order all the services and goods. I worked there for 6 months and am going on a second rotation next spring while I am in my last semester at my university. The position has engagingly fit my education. I am a Supply Chain Management major, so I have a background in purchasing as well as finance and a lot of supply chain. This position is a mix of all these experiences, with a heavy focus on supply relation and process improvement. Past classes have definitely helped me understand this always evolving and completely hybrid job. I am not an expert in finance, and although this co-op is a finance co-op, the expectation to be very well versed in finance is low.

The company is a smaller pharma company, only employing about 575 people currently. When the company was smaller, this position was a one-person job, and the procurement expertise area is only 3 years old. As the company grows, the group grows, and as the group grows, it becomes more necessary. This still private and has not commercialized any drugs yet. This has allowed procurement to prove its importance and value to the company through implementing entry, requesting, buying, and related processes. SAP was recently implemented to expand the group's power in creating POs and documenting our financials from purchases. Procurement holds extraordinary value to the company by sourcing the best mix of products whether that is the best value item or the item that will improve relations with a vendor. New saving goals were implemented, the creation of an RFQ (request for quote) system and a project tracking system were all implemented to give procurement the best tools to support the business. Procurement supports the business on two ends; acting as the customer to vendors and reaching for great deals while also working as customer service providers to those within the company and making purchasing and negotiations very simple. The group hires not only one co-op, but two, in hopes of creating a senior and junior co-op. This has allowed the group to expand and distribute workload more evenly allowing the senior co-op to work on more projects and the junior co-op to work on transactional data to support the purchasing. This co-op program has been around for five years, and every cycle has been light years different just from the constant growth of the company.

The company just held their yearly "State of the State" all day meeting to discuss plans and decisions they are looking to make in the next year. From this meeting came a very specific "Challenge Accepted" mantra. It refers to the current goal of having three commercialized drugs by 2020 in the therapeutic field. It also relates to the constant struggle that many small pharmaceutical companies go through of being bought up and absorbed by smaller companies. Many collaborations and partnerships have been created to support an independent company that is working to grow and fit the need of the market and patients before looking into mergers or acquisitions of any kind.

Currently, my company is around 575 people, seeking to add 1,200 employees by 2020. All of these growth plans for the size of the company profoundly reflect the plan to have three late phases, commercialize drugs on the market by 2020. The company culture is critical to my business because it creates its structure. Basically, the culture builds the company. We are very decentralized, allowing fluidity and flexibility in every department. Each area breaks up into expertise areas and has very focused, a small team to take on certain tasks needed for the business. This allows us to decrease red tape and create a culture of "small business" in a larger, growing business. The commitment level to co-ops is unlike I have heard or seen from most companies. There are always a large number of co-ops that join the company across all expertise areas including chemistry, quality control, procurement, finance, and HR. It is a standard joke around the company that once you start working here, you never leave. It's like a black hole. It has been amazing to see how many co-ops look to come back for more co-ops and extending into the future for full-time positions. It shows that the commitment we have to co-ops is robust enough to bring many of them back to stay. It is easy to be a co-op at the company and forget you are only there for 6 months. A lot of responsibility and pressure is put on co-ops to do well but is strongly supported by the managers and leaders who have been involved in this program for years.

My position supported the business. I was there to allow that the science of the organization ran smoothly through ensuring materials and services were always available when needed. As procurement and finance, you need to support the main business, which was drug development and work to solve, mitigate, and decrease any problems that may bottleneck this process. The scientists are not able to complete their experiments if we cannot order and deliver the goods they need. The packaging for the drugs cannot be created if we do not negotiate terms with a company to service the packaging and labeling of these drugs. It is interesting to be in a position that is not the focus of the company, but it is great to learn how to be the supporting pillars of such a great organization.

The primary focus for 2017 in our group was savings. We are tasked with a huge savings goal that is distributed among the buyers. Between the two co-ops, one full-time buyer, and one full-time buyer who is split between our department and clinical testing and contracts we must save or avoid $60,000 each. Although this is a specific goal for 2017, it displays the focus on hitting marks and making tangible and accountable goals. There is a system in place that we just implemented that tracks our projects across the entire business. We must enter our projects and what we're working on into the system, set timelines, goals, reasons why this is worth our time, rankings, and participants. The savings goal is simply a small part of the larger goal of our area to track progress and success and hold you and other's accountable for work. This has affected the projects I am working on such as trying to reach savings goals and entering in RFQs to choose suppliers for certain items. I have made it a personal goal to hit every timeline I set in this new system without modifying them. Since our area focuses on hitting deadlines, I felt it necessary to make myself accountable to the group. This was a challenge, as you cannot account for sudden meetings, re-prioritizing projects, or day-to-day changes that can set you back. That is a general challenge the group faced since we were always tracking our progress it was hard sometimes to prioritize our projects.

My day-to-day activities shifted substantially from month 1 to month 6. In the first month, the position required a lot of transactional work. It was very data entry based and allowed me as a co-op to learn the business slowly and know what the position needed on the most basic level. As time moved on, the position shifted to be about 50% data entry, 25% customer service reach out which included servicing the customers, and 25% projects which included requests for quotes, reports on spend analysis, and supplier selection in the vendors we ordered from. As the position has shifted, my day-to-day activities have moved to include data entry into our ordering system, calling vendors to fix issues with orders, and working with the team to determine new projects to peruse and work on to better the company.

The job description for this role was very minimal. "A buyer for goods within an R&D pharmaceutical company," I think was the description. It was really what you wanted to make of it and what you pursued to create for yourself and provide to your manager or group to better the company. The standard requirements needed for the job and expected were to be skilled in Excel, enter data from system to system easily, work well with customers but also work hard as a customer, and find opportunities in the business to save money. How you interpreted these tasks was up to each individual. I have been able to expand my experience and create these projects such as creating a Request for Proposal (RFP), going through supplier selection, creating business profiles for executives to review and pick vendors, evaluate and test new systems for the company such as SMART by GEP, SAP, and Oracle. These are all projects I would not have typically been handed unless I asked and expressed interest in. There is a lot to learn from the saying, "you don't know the answer until you ask."

I took on a few projects that required high teamwork capabilities. The biggest was an RFP that required three of the team members to collaborate on the wording of questions, requirements for the information needed, and suppliers we were going to select. This team also constituted of two scientists and one manager lead, totaling six people on the team. The scientists were necessary because to create a requirements sheet for the chemicals we were looking to source. We needed their input on the types of machines they used and the current chemical requirements they had. The manager lead was well versed in supplier negotiations and a great project manager, which helped to facilitate timelines and due dates for the team. This team project was started and finished within a month, so it was a fast turnaround that required a lot of long, detailed meetings to hit all the requirements within the timeline. I was able to see that managing projects was easy but managing people was hard.

My job was not as focused on technical functions, but it was necessary to hold certain skills that allowed you to network through the business correctly. One major technical function of my position was working Excel. Many of our projects were Excel based, and it was easier to manipulate data within Excel since a majority of it was price based. By honing Excel skills, it was simpler to operate the position and take advantage of everything it had to offer which was recognizing savings opportunities or noticing gaps in data that allowed us to negotiate with vendors. Another technical function was working SAP. The company implemented SAP a little over a year ago, and it has been a very long road to getting users comfortable with the system. By becoming skilled at SAP, you are, once again, able to take advantage of all the best aspects of the position and business by examining data, changing data to fix problems, or running reports that show data to give way to more opportunities for savings. The ability to gain and master these two technical functions of the position was crucial for the success as well as happiness within the job.

Since some of my projects were somewhat specific to Supply Chain or Finance, there were some classes and academic background that were necessary to my success in completing these projects. Although some of these projects were helpful to have academic qualifications, the projects are highly based on relationship and knowledge of the business that can be gained with time. It is necessary for this position to understand basic business which is quickly learned through beginning level classes your freshman and sophomore year. I had to pick up on more finance terms than I was used to and I was able to reference back to notes I kept from years before to help. But, now with everything at your fingertips, self-taught success is not unheard of. I have almost no science background and entering this position at a pharmaceutical company came to be a shock. I had to research what certain lab suppliers were so I could negotiate deals with vendors. I had to understand what types of chemicals were corrosive so I was able to reach out to the business and inform them we needed specialized packaging to transport the chemicals. It all came with research and drive, which was slightly supported by prior academic learning but was not the foundation. My projects were analytical and relationship based in nature that allowed me to learn a lot on the job and did not require substantial knowledge of finance, supply chain, biology, or chemistry.

There were main goals set for savings such as hitting the $60,000 savings goal by the end of my 6-month co-op. Other targets included reducing unpredictable and expensive vendors and gaining more business with reliable, cheap suppliers. This was measured by how many vendors I was able to eliminate and how much business, in dollars, I was able to move to better vendors. Again, goals were focused on tangible, achievable aspects of the business.

Many projects were focused on SMART by GEP and SAP. SMART by GEP tracked spend over the past 3 years of the business, projects we had in the pipeline, and RFPs/RFIs/RFQs we were working on to send to vendors. SAP allowed us to run reports on what items we were ordering and all the documents we made to send to the suppliers (Purchase Orders and Purchase Requisitions). SAP generated key data we pulled into GEP to analyze and view. Both systems were necessary to complete a full analysis of the business. As for formulas, the only time we had to reference formulas was when we created business profiles for vendors to present to executives in the company. These profiles would include qualitative and quantitative data for members to evaluate and judge vendors on. In these profiles, there was a financial section that we had to plug 10K and financial statement data into to get numbers such as Operating Cash Flow, Z Scores, and etc. These formulas were best entered into Excel once then re-visited as needed when new vendors were requested.

For spend data when evaluating what savings were possible between certain vendors, it was important to analyze the percentage of spend we had with the vendor across the entire business, what percentage of spending we do with them for that individual project, and what percentage increases they had with that product over a few years span. This allowed our buying unit to fairly judge and evaluate what amount of money vendors were overcharging us or what deals we were actually getting based on past data. With this analysis, we could take it and apply it to negotiations and conversations with vendors about the overall business. As the company is a growing business, it was always crucial to present to vendors that we are looking to drastically expand business from now until 2020 when we plan to go commercial. Numbers were not present to give to vendors about how much the business would increase, but that is something possible to show as the time gets closer to increase savings and decrease risk with vendors and products and services.

I was responsible for making a 1400 lined Excel sheet that presented all the contracts we had with consultants. What projects they were involved in, how many years of experience they had, how many years/months they had worked with The company, their hourly rates, how many people they had on their team and how on track their projects were. This was one of my biggest and most daunting projects to complete as it was being presented to the president to show what consultants we wanted to cancel contracts with and what consultants we could move to other projects if we wanted. It was very transactional and very dense, requiring me to work in one system that held all of our contracts, Statements of Work (SOWs) and Change Orders (COs). I was then tasked with presenting an RFI to the group that showed why we should switch our business from one vendor management software to another. This required me to gather information from six vendors and compare them across the entire business, not just focusing on the price of the software but also recognizing the ease of use, training necessary to use it, and integration with other systems. This presentation was over a month's time with enough time to prepare and gather the best information.

I was given a very good review during my time at the company. My two peers, as well as both of my bosses, have reviewed me. I have not received a written review yet from my manager who is responsible for the university review. I made it a point to have check-in meetings with one of my full-time co-workers as well as my manager three separate times to get feedback on my work and progress in the position. Each time I was able to receive great feedback on what I needed to work on and what I was doing well. My latest meeting with my manager allowed me to notice I don't do a great job at delegating my work when I am overbooked with projects or daily work but I am a team player who is always willing to help others with their job. There were moments I would have benefited to ask for help and reach out, but instead kept to myself and completed to work but in a much slower fashion than if I passed the work off to someone else. The feedback was always constructive and helped each time I received it. I do not like to suck up or present myself as an annoyance to my co-workers or bosses which my colleague noted can hurt me sometimes because those other workers who show enthusiasm in the workplace and reach out to their bosses and ask more questions usually are pulled into projects or opportunities. As the written evaluation has not been given yet, I will be very interested and very receptive to what my manager has to say. I imagine it to be good since I will still continue to work there in the fall and spring and hopefully after graduation.

This job made significant contributions to my career development and growth. I was able to work in a part of Supply Chain and Finance that was not just business but was mixed with science and healthcare. As I had never seen this type of business before I am very grateful I was exposed to it early in my career as I feel it is the right fit for me. This position has supplied me with exceptional hard skills in SAP and GEP software, which is very rare for an entry-level position at any company. It has helped me grow and become a strong and independent young female in the workplace as well. Being able to negotiate terms of a contract and prices with, in more cases than one, an older male, has given me an immense sense of pride and accomplishment in the workplace. It has shown me that my goals of being a very successful female executive at a company can start now. My career was able to grow at this company by working through problems and being trusted in finding solutions others couldn't. Gaining exposure to different types of business and with various kinds of people is just an important to me in career development than learning hard skills.

As I will be a fifth-year senior, after this co-op my time to choose coursework at the university is limited. But with the few classes, I can still pick I will be more drawn to healthcare or science fields of business, if offered, compared to other classes. The combination of business and healthcare is intriguing and is a tough topic to address in current political situations and being involved directly in an area that is finance and healthcare have made me appreciate more about the healthcare industry than before. I have also been drawn to apply to more graduate programs before. Now, I am interested in looking into a broader business focus rather than just supply chain.

The most applicable course was Purchasing and Procurement. That was the most similar to my co-op by far since I was in the Finance and Procurement expertise area. We studied a lot about negotiating tactics and different aspects of RFPs, which helped me immensely in my projects and work with vendors. Another course that was exceedingly helpful was Organizational Behavior This class was able to prepare me for moments in the workplace a textbook does not prepare you for. One example of this is learning about company culture, and more specifically how companies allow their employees to be their authentic selves. The company's culture focuses on the individual and comfort of the person within the enterprise. My co-workers, none of which look the same, act the same, dress the same, or are from any of the same places, all get along and are happy together due to their abilities to express their authentic selves. I am now able to understand why I am happy at this workplace and why so many other people are happy. Being your true self is not taught from a textbook but seen through example and appreciated when experienced in real life.

The biggest distinction is no one tells you how hard it really is. Working day in and day out without much variation is a tough thing to do, and I don't believe anyone relays to people entering the workforce what it is like. It is often depicted as 'a new chapter in your life' instead of being presented as a hard change in your life you must be committed to making. Particularly for people who are new to the workforce, it is hard to prepare them for the politics of the workplace, the unspoken rules and expectations, the long hours, and the change from college. My education has been fantastic at the university. Something I feel I would be unable to replicate at any other school, however that includes the on-the job-experiences I have had during my three years here. The real-world experiences have made the ease of finding a job that much greater and the nerves of joining the workforce that much smaller. I was able to gain much more useful knowledge working two co-ops than I would have gained if I were in classes those semesters. On co-op, you learn the nuances of office politics, which is almost impossible to teach in the classroom. On co-op, you learn about consequences of coming in late, not finishing projects on time or disappointing your boss(es) which you will almost never learn with a teacher. These small, but significant distinctions make the on-the-job experience a hundred times more useful than class time in my opinion.

I think my co-op built my technical background. It is rare you are put into a class where you can build your own RFP in software or create POs with real money to send to vendors or manipulate data to analyze and report to create savings goals. I credit almost all of my technical background to my past two co-ops where I have learned to increase my Excel skills and gain skills in Oracle, Query Studio, SAP, and GEP.

I am delighted with my co-op. I would recommend it to many other students to try and take if given a chance. It is a great combination of business, both finance and supply chain, and science and healthcare. Being a part of a company that pushes their co-ops to take on more responsibilities and grows their career from day one is an environment that al co-ops should be in at least once. With the company growing, the opportunities grow as well. I have been able to gain valuable technical skills and create and improve soft competencies in a short period of six months. An experience like this at another company is rare in my opinion.

I think there should have been a more centralized co-op mentor program meaning a more point person for the co-ops to go to and ask questions to or get feedback from. Since our team was small, everyone was beyond busy which didn't always allow time for feedback from the co-op manager. This would have been really useful since the co-ops were handed large responsibilities early on. It was a good way to prepare for full-time work, but guidance would have made the co-op experience that much better if included.

CHAPTER 5

MARKETING

If you'd like to put your creative nature to use in the marketing, advertising, and PR sector, you'll need some relevant work experience, and some useful contacts marketing, advertising and public relations (PR) exist in most businesses and across all sectors. People working in this area help organizations to connect with their audiences and promote brands, products, and messages. You could work in PR, advertising, market research, brand management, direct marketing, event management, sales promotion, or marketing communications (online marketing and social media).

WHAT DO EMPLOYERS LOOK FOR?

It's not necessary to have a related degree, as companies often look for skills rather than specific subjects. Employees who've studied courses that require creativity and excellent communication skills often find that their abilities fit these roles. However, a degree in PR, marketing, media, advertising, journalism, communications or event management will demonstrate an interest in the industry and may prove to be an advantage in an increasingly competitive area.

Design positions in advertising may specify an art and design degree. Employers generally require candidates with: a good understanding of social media and digital marketing; commercial awareness and financial understanding; communication skills; creativity and innovation; customer service skills; and numerical and analytical skills.

HOW DO I FIND A JOB?

Getting employment in this area can be difficult as most employers don't require candidates to have related degrees, meaning that vacancies can be open to all graduates. One way to find jobs is to create and maintain a profile on LinkedIn. Many companies use social media to advertise their entry-level opportunities and also promote their vacancies through careers fairs and university careers services. Make sure that you regularly check the Facebook, LinkedIn and Twitter pages of marketing-related companies.

There's no standard application process in advertising, and vacancies are often filled by word of mouth, so making speculative applications is essential. It's important to build up a network of contacts, as smaller businesses may use informal recruitment practices to find candidates. Check marketing agency websites early in the academic year to find information on entry-level or management training schemes and deadlines.

WHAT'S THE WORKING CULTURE?

Graduates can expect:

- Salaries to vary widely depending on the role, the type of organization you work for and the area of the country where you are based.
- To be in a dynamic team with a sociable atmosphere.
- Working hours of generally 9am to 5pm, Monday to Friday, though longer hours may be required to meet deadlines and attend events.

CO-OP PARTICIPANT INTERVIEWS

Interviewee #1 of 4

For my most recent co-op, I worked for a company as the Retail Marketing co-op. When I began my co-op, our office was located in in the suburbs, and halfway through my time there we moved into a new office in the city. This co-op had a good mix of connecting to my education, while also connecting to my personal interests and previous professional experience. As a Business Administration and Interactive Media major, this position gave me the opportunity to serve in an interdisciplinary role from a business and creative sense, interacting and getting real experience with both teams. Additionally, I have always had a keen personal interest in apparel and retail, and have worked at a clothing startup, Ministry of Supply, for the past three years. This gave me the opportunity to see the internal operations of a much larger company in a similar industry.

I believe that my role had considerable value to the organization despite being a temporary position. Much of the monthly work was cyclical, so once my feet were wet, I was thrown into the execution side of a majority of the monthly work, while my manager was able to focus on more strategic decisions. The company has had co-ops in the past, but typically only hires one at a time. Since a majority of the work that needs to take place in a footwear retail company is marketing-based, the role of the Retail Marketing co-op was significant. They typically hire co-ops that are passionate about the industry, have an eye for design, and are able to understand data collection and data-driven decision-making. Additionally, my background in Interactive Media made me an attractive hire because I had a lot of technical experience that was unique to anyone in my department at any level.

The company has a little over 15,000 employees and employs a mix of corporate workers as well as a global retail customer-facing staff. The headquarters is located in outside of the United States but has an American HQ. The company hires many people of many different professional, educational, and demographic backgrounds, and has a very unique family-orientation for such a large corporation. It was not uncommon to run into multiple members of the same family that worked at the company.

My role fits into the organization because retail marketing was one of the most crucial areas to execute in for the company. Additionally, my interdisciplinary skillset put me in the position to interact and work with many different teams, from Creative to Wholesale, to Digital, and even Product.

The company exists in a very competitive market and one in which technological innovation and unique, proactive aesthetic were becoming more successful. Footwear was also pushing into a more sneaker-oriented direction. This was a huge challenge for the company, a heritage company with a classic aesthetic rooted in more formal situations. As a marketing team, we had to manage to appear cool and innovative to younger consumers without alienating our existing, older client base that was still a significant portion of the market but was ultimately going to phase out. Additionally, the company didn't have much of an online presence and was not using data in any marketing decisions to that point. As such, given my personal interest and interdisciplinary experience, my opinion held a lot of weight in discussions involving younger consumers.

Additionally, I was put in charge of a store survey project, in which I had to communicate with all of our retail and outlet locations to learn about the physical layout of the stores, which tables/and other furniture items each store contained. With this data, we were able to combine it with sales data and get a better picture of how to lay out the design of our stores for success. Also, it helped us get every store standardized to support when we made monthly alterations to the visual merchandising company-wide.

My specific day-to-day responsibilities included, going to creative status meetings to be briefed and give input on the progress on projects related to signage, digital, and print ads with the marketing and creative teams. The bulk of my work came from creating distribution lists for store signage and fixtures for given campaigns or seasonal promotions, and then creating visual merchandising planners for product mix and layout in stores to drive sales and appropriately tell product stories to customers. There was much traveling involved in this role, as I was consistently traveling to stores to see through the implementation of marketing initiatives or testing potential visual merchandising changes in an actual store environment.

Additionally, there was internal work, like coordinating product orders for marketing or creative teams, ordering fixtures and signage for stores, and some administrative and customer service work. A lot of the duties I took on in addition to my role involved working with the creative team. Having a background in both business and creative, my skillset could be leveraged as a liaison or translator between both teams. It also saved time for both teams, in situations where the marketing team needed smaller things done and the creative team was already busy, I could do the necessary creative work for marketing to move forward. Lastly, my pushing past the role came was more of a process innovation than anything else.

Before my start at the company, one member of the marketing department created all store visual merchandising planners in Adobe InDesign. This was a substantial and time-consuming task, which took place on a consistent basis of at least once a month. What made this most difficult was that nobody in the department had a real background in Adobe InDesign, and it was time-consuming to edit and update each time as a result. When put in charge of the visual merchandising planners on my co-op, I realized that we weren't necessarily leveraging InDesign for what it's best used for, but it seemed like we were using it because it was the flashiest program for getting the job done. Instead, I opted to use PowerPoint, because it would be easier to use an update for the future and almost everyone has used PowerPoint at some point. I was able to produce these planners at a far faster rate than could be done in the past, and the company marketing department still uses my template to this day. A lot of the projects that I worked on were around collecting data about customers, but the stores themselves as well. With a vast network of stores and a company that has been around longer than computers, a lot of data has been lost in the shuffle, and the company had been afforded the luxury of being able to succeed without it.

As data continues to be of critical importance to businesses, we wanted to make sure we had an accurate understanding of the layout of all of our stores, what fixtures they contained, and what signage they had. This involved many trips to stores, emails and phone calls, and a survey project coordinated with the field to get that understanding. It was a lot of legwork to be done while other strategic decisions had to take place concurrently, so I believe this is why I was given so much responsibility here. The data was then used to standardize the signage and fixture inventory and assist in accurately creating signage distribution lists, which saved the company significant money in shipping and printing signage.

Much to my pleasure, my supervisor and the team at-large had a positive assessment of my work upon my leaving my co-op at the company. Through the co-op program's evaluation system, I was given clear feedback on where I was successful, where I still have room for professional growth and my overall performance in the role. Thankfully it was overwhelmingly positive, and the department extended my stay for another month and a half until I had to return to classes, and began discussions about a potential post-grad return to the team. As much as I'd like to say that my success was entirely my own doing, I believe my colleagues at the company and the company environment had a large contribution to my success there. The team was very open with each other, for better or for worse, and that open communication always drove progress. As a result of my co-op experience, I did have a clearer idea of some areas that I wanted to learn more about. I became much more interested in data analytics and technology.

Unfortunately, due to rigid program structure, I wasn't able to learn more about them through coursework, but I have been able to pursue them through extracurricular activities and online programs provided by the school. It has, however, guided my course selection process around what I think would be more professionally applicable in a way that I hadn't done in the past. I now think about which courses will give me hard interdisciplinary skills or classes that will allow me to be agile and solve problems from a different perspective. I now have a far greater appreciation for my design classes, because thinking like a designer has allowed me to address the issues in a way that I would not have been able to with strictly a business background.

As a result, I have taken some psychology classes that have given me a better understanding of what motivates people, or how to best interact with different types of individuals. I think this has been one of the more valuable lessons I've learned, along with taking classes that give technical skills like finance, accounting, or computer skills. My co-op experience certainly helped shape my class selection process around becoming better rounded and agile, as well as being a better communicator. My co-op definitely made use of my design background, but in a much different way than my classwork has. Previously, I had no professional design experience, and all of my work was centered on school projects, or doing cool projects with my free time. On co-op, my design experience was leveraged in short-term internal situations or for far less exciting applications like marketing communications.

All in all, my co-op experience was a precious one. There was a lot of responsibility that I was allowed to run with, and I think that's exactly what I needed to push myself on my second co-op. I benefited from it, and I believe the department benefited from a fresh perspective. I would certainly recommend it to anyone with a passion for the apparel, footwear, or retail industry because it was an opportunity to see how an organization carries out its operations that may not have been available to me through a more traditional pathway. If I could improve anything about the role, I would have the co-op do more presentations or public speaking, because I believe that's a crucial professional skill that students should master going into the working world. I also would provide more structured opportunities for mentoring, and learning new technical skills.

Interviewee #2 of 4

For my second co-op experience, I worked at an investment management firm based in the city's financial district, as the Media Relations co-op. My co-op coordinator recommended this co-op position to me, and I was unsure of whether it would be a good fit for me. After about a week in which both a phone interview and an in-person interview took place, I was offered the position. I received an offer from another company shortly after and had to weigh the pros and cons of each position. Ultimately, I opted to work at the firm because I had the opportunity to meet members of my team in person during the interview process and had a sense of what the job entailed by being able to speak with the current co-op student. Whereas the only information I had about the other firm and their position for me was based on a brief phone interview. I was very pleased with my decision to join the firm because I knew it would push me to achieve my professional goals. More importantly, it introduced me to a new potential career path within marketing, consisting of media and PR work, which I may never have considered without this experience.

Based on my experience at the company, I can think of examples where my co-workers or my team demonstrated the importance of integrity, teamwork, creativity, and professionalism. As a co-op, these core values were brought to my attention during the introductory courses (discussed later) for all co-ops, interns, and new employees. They stressed the importance of us adopting these core values as members of the firm community to both be respectful in the workplace and help the company as a whole strive for excellence. In all honesty, I probably would not have been able to list these values off the top of my head by the end of my experience, not because I had forgotten what they were, but because I would have considered other values learned along the way to be just as important.

As the Media Relations co-op I was part of the Media Relations team that consisted of three people: The Director of Media Relations, the Media Relations Manager, and myself. Although the manager was my direct supervisor, I reported to, accepted assignments from, and worked closely with both the manager and the director. My responsibilities mostly consisted of day-to-day tasks and assisting my team members in their projects. Over time, I believe I was given greater responsibility by providing larger and more major contributions to all of the projects the media team had taken on. In addition to these growing responsibilities, I managed to continue the day-to-day tasks by finding new, innovative ways to get them done quickly and efficiently.

The Media Relations team was responsible for sharing news and information about the company and its employees appropriately both internally and externally. We worked hard to come up with several types of communication strategies that would best deliver accurate information to a specified audience. Whether they were internal emails that were strictly for employees or press releases that would be released to various journalists and the public, everything required specific formatting and language that was tailored to the intended audience while still being representable of the company's image. I think our role in the company was a significant one because it was our duty to ensure that every interaction between the company and the media, such as a television interview, a press release, survey results, and so on, represented the firm in the best way possible.

During my time at the company, the firm had roughly 18 co-op students from two different universities. These co-op students had various majors and were mainly divided among the marketing, accounting, and investment teams. Additionally, the firm offered internship programs ranging from 10 weeks to 4 months in various departments.

Duties

The interview process for the Media Relations position went as follows:

- My co-op coordinator at my university submitted my resume to the employer after I expressed interest in the position using the co-op job board at my university.
- An HR representative from the firm reached out by both phone and email to set up a phone call with me.
- A short phone call took place with her and then we discussed my availability to come in for an in-person interview.
- At the office, I met with the HR representative briefly. Afterwards, I met with the current co-op student and her current manager, the Media Relations Manager (she would become my future boss). At the time of my interview, the

director was out of the country for business, so I only met her the day I started working.

- The hiring manager reached out to me about three business days later to offer me the position.

The job description outlined several requirements for this position such as communication skills, organizational skills, detail-oriented, basic computer skills and general professionalism. I felt that I could mostly rely on the professional skills I acquired during my first co-op experience as the Marketing and Events co-op at my university, but it became apparent that I would also learn a lot on the job. A basic understanding of the finance industry and investment management was not necessary but was certainly beneficial. I had learned briefly about stocks, bonds, trades, and investment tools and tactics in my Financial Management course, yet because of my marketing concentration, I haven't taken any other courses relating to finance. The majority of what I learned about investment management was based on a few impromptu crash courses taught by my supervisor in our initial meetings during my first week on the job. General marketing and business concepts that I learned while in classes also proved to be useful on occasion. For the most part, however, the position was more of a 'learn as you go' type of job.

While I was expected to have basic computer skills and be proficient in general computer applications such as MS Word, PowerPoint, Excel, and Outlook, training was offered for all company-specific programs and a number of proprietary tools. My team did a superb job making sure I attended the appropriate training sessions and was capable of using the programs I was likely to face in my position. In addition to computer application training, all of the co-op students took part in several training sessions and introductory courses, described below:

- We had to take a course entitled "Mutual Fund Industry Overview." This course included three sessions in which an HR manager taught us the basics investment management in the financial industry and how the firm specifically fit into that industry.
- Another course taught by the same HR employee was entitled "How to Be Successful in the Workplace." In this course, the co-op students were taught how to behave, communicate, and dress appropriately and respectfully in the workplace. Additionally, it gave us a better insight into the environment and culture we were likely to experience while working at the firm.
- Safety seminar and data recovery training were also offered. This session outlined what employees are expected to do in any type of emergency. We were also informed about how and where the company's data is stored and backed up.
- All co-op students, as well as new full-time employees, had to partake in Harassment Awareness Training. Due to scheduling conflicts, the co-op students were unable to attend a class specifically designed for this training. Instead, we all completed an online training session, the purpose of which was to inform us of how to identify and report any form of harassment occurring in the office.
- (Not for all co-ops) The Media Relations team outlines the preparation process for live television interviews. This included training in setting up the in-house camera, lights, table, backdrop, microphone and earpiece set.

For this position, my responsibilities included the following:

- 'The Firm in the News' was a daily task in which I would search for and compile news articles that mentioned Eaton Vance or featured spokespeople from the company. This compilation would be sent out by email every day to 700+ employees. Afterward, I would save the stories and video or radio clips to be archived by the company. The goal of "The Firm In The News" and general press coverage is to spread positive and imperative information about the company both internally and externally.

- Another daily task included tracking and documenting pending, published, declined, or canceled press inquiries. Published work would be saved in an Excel spreadsheet and sent out in 'The Firm In The News' while all other potential interviews would be tracked using a proprietary program. It was my responsibility to keep the internal systems up to date by giving each entry as much detail as possible (i.e., journalist name, news outlet, type of interview, date and time of interview, spokesperson requested, etc.)

- I would regularly assist in the scheduling and set up of interviews, which could be in person, over phone, TV, or radio, between the press and the firm employees. For live television interviews, I would be in charge of reaching out to the third-party company that controlled the office camera remotely to make them aware of the interview details. My team would work with this company to connect the spokesperson from our office in the city to be broadcast on the appropriate network (such as CNBC or Bloomberg TV) for their interview. Occasionally, the interviewee would fly to New York to do an in-studio interview, however, having the camera in the office was extremely useful for last minute interview requests.

- At the end of each week, I created a summary of the media team's progress in ongoing projects and media outreach. This summary, which I put together as both a Word document and an Excel spreadsheet, was sent along with all other department updates to be revised by the CEO and department heads. This gave managers the opportunity to stay updated with all levels of the organization and make sure sufficient communication was occurring between various teams.

- On a quarterly basis, I updated and published the company's national and international corporate profiles (see attached). My manager and I would work together to reach out to various departments to receive the appropriate data. I would then work with the design team in the marketing department to make these changes. Finally, I would upload the updated versions of the profiles to the company's website via a program called Media Manager.

- Occasionally, I drafted and distributed press releases and media advisories to managed media contacts and targeted press lists. These works often went through several revisions before being published. The press releases varied from quarterly earnings summaries to the results of the proprietary survey. The media advisories (that I worked on) usually summarized the thoughts and opinions of our portfolio managers on the current market news, such as the Federal Reserve meeting and changing interest rates.

- I also helped organize and schedule a Choices, Challenges, and Careers (CCC) event with firm executives. The CCC lunches were events open to all employees that consisted of a brief presentation followed by QA with representatives from specific departments in the company. For the spring quarter, my team and I worked with the IT department who presented the importance of security and data sharing within the company. They also discussed current tech trends that were likely to impact how business is conducted in the financial industry and specifically at the firm.

- Lastly, I supported the development of a quarterly survey sent to financial advisors nationwide, by assisting in questionnaire development and data analysis, creating marketing materials (see attached), and promoting the results to reporters and media outlets. The survey focused on revealing which of the four key issues (income, taxes, volatility, and growth) were "top-of-mind" for financial advisors. Additionally, the survey questions inquired about the strategies and tools used by financial advisors to adhere to their clients' needs. The overall goal of the survey was to gain a better understanding of financial advisors; what information they knew, what tools they were using with their clients, the types of relationships they would establish with their clients, what information they were most interested in, and so on.

Supporting the creation of survey was a very enjoyable experience but not something I initially thought would be one of my responsibilities. I do not recall the need to create a proprietary survey appearing in the job description. However, there was some reference to assisting with "special projects." Despite having little to no experience with survey development, my manager (the Media Relations Manager) did an excellent job easing me into the process and making sure I was included as a contributing member of the survey team. The core group mainly consisted of people from the marketing department with specified responsibilities such as designing the graphics, writing content for promotional materials, posting results to social media, and so on. Additionally, we worked with a managing director who became the lead spokesperson for survey. His opinions, as well as reactions from other directors and portfolio managers in the company, were showcased in the summary report, a packet created to summarize the survey results using a story, graphics, and statistics. The survey itself was generated and distributed by a third-party company. This company would also collect the responses and send us back the statistics for every single question. They even could separate responses based on respondent demographics. We all worked together to develop the questionnaire and essentially create a story to be picked up by the media based on the results. Not only did the survey provide us with a better understanding of financial advisors and their clients, but it also created an opportunity for more press coverage.

As I had previously mentioned, I was not expecting to be a part of the survey project. It was still relatively new when I joined, only having launched a few years earlier, which meant that the process lacked a strict timeline and there were few expectations for the quarterly results. Seeing the entire process all the way through, however, was an incredible experience and has sparked an interest to pursue market research. Of course, I still haven't decided on a strict career path, but without this project, I may never have considered market research to be a possibility. My university offers a market research course that I had already taken as a requirement for my major. While the class had its interesting moments, I also found it to be somewhat repetitive since we focused mainly on how to work with one particular program (SPSS). Additionally, the class did not offer a lot of insight into how market research can be used in the real world, such as in the financial industry. Instead, we created surveys for college students to be analyzed by a college student, the results of which were then presented to college students. I believe this is a perfect example of why co-op is such an important experience for students. What we learn in class can't actually be understood, or even appreciated, until we encounter it in the real world.

The co-op department requested that toward the end of the co-op experience both my supervisor and I complete assessments individually and then discuss our responses with one another. In this evaluation, I evaluated the position, my team, the company as a whole, and my perceived performance during this co-op experience. My manager assessed the co-op process and my performance as well. For the most part, our assessment of my performance fell in line with one another. We both agreed that I became more comfortable in my position and gained more confidence when faced with greater responsibility or when working with employees from other departments and teams. Based on her assessment, it had become apparent to my manager that I preferred to work alone. While I do not necessarily agree, I can see why she had made this conclusion. There were several tasks and projects in which we collaborated with other employees, both in and outside the marketing department, but in these situations, I was always with another member of my team. Looking back, I realize I made little effort to reach out to other teams on my own terms. If I had been encouraged to do so, I think I would have appreciated the opportunity to explore other teams and departments to get a sense of their responsibilities and contribution to the company's success.

I believe this co-op experience helped me grow in my professional career. My specific goals at the time were to improve my time management and organizational skills, which I believe I achieved. Additionally, I wanted to become more confident in my ability to lead projects or tasks and manage others. I reached this to a certain extent, as there were not many opportunities to fully embrace a leadership position. However, I often felt I had the trust and respect from several of my co-workers to take on projects that required a greater level of responsibility over time. Another goal was to gain a better understanding of the financial industry. Once again, I achieved this to a certain extent. Although finance is not my forte, I learned throughout this experience that I could still be successful if I choose to work in this type of industry. As I mentioned earlier, there is a significant difference between learning about a concept in class and experiencing it in the workforce. I learned first-hand that just because you don't enjoy a class or don't particularly do well in it, doesn't mean it is not a suitable career path. For example, I had to take a Financial Management course, which I found extremely difficult, but I still managed to work successfully and gain a lot from my experience in a financial management firm.

Overall, I thought this co-op was an excellent experience. I was able to utilize and expand my professional skillset while learning a lot about an industry I had never considered working in. I gained a deeper understanding of what it means to work in a corporate setting by being exposed to corporate office culture and witnessing how each employee, team, and department contributes to the company's overall mission. I would certainly recommend this co-op to a first or second-timer student studying marketing, communications, or journalism. I know that co-op student's responsibilities change from cycle to cycle and are tailored to the student's specific capabilities. With that said, I cannot provide detailed recommendations for improvements because it really does depend on what the student brings to the table. If I were to return to the role, I, personally, would love to be involved in more interdepartmental projects to expose myself to different areas of the company. All in all, it was tremendous co-op experience that ultimately revealed what I should be looking for in a career.

Interviewee #3 of 4

I am currently going into my last year at my university. I am a dual concentration in Marketing and Management Information Systems with a minor in Criminal Justice. I have done two co-ops so far and will be going on my third and final one this upcoming summer. My first co-op I completed was a company located in the city. I completed my co-op there but then was asked to come back and work part-time. My title there was Sales Associate and consisted mostly of customer service for their implants and various products sold. My most recent co-op completed was working for the company in the role of a Food and Drug Sales Analyst.

The company, in general, is known for hiring different interns and co-ops through various programs similar to and including the university program. The organization, the branch I worked for specifically, tends to take on a few different co-ops from my university at various locations including the headquarters in Midwest and other places across the country. The organization has been participating in co-op programs for many years. During my co-op, I was the only student from my university that went to the Midwest location.

However, they were other interns/co-ops there hired from local colleges in the Midwest working there. They also have this leadership program that's two years and can apply for after graduating college. From what I was told, the organization encourages hiring co-ops to bring in young, new talent. One of the ladies that worked in Finance said that the co-op is the organization's way of dating you first before seeing if they like you enough to bring on full-time. She also told me that it should be a 2-way date, meaning I should be 'dating' the company as well and seeing if I like/fit into the culture. The organization enjoys bringing back people who have done co-ops/internships with them since they don't have to re-train or teach stuff and like bringing back people who have already proved themselves within the company.

The organization has a total of about 17,000 employees. At the headquarters where I worked in the Midwest, we had about 600 employees at the site. Employees on site at headquarters included most of the high up management level positions including the CEO, CFO, and CMO. They typically assign co-ops to different managers at that are on site at the park. My supervisor in specific was in charge of the entire sales team at the organization, both the West and East

Coast. My position, while labeled Food and Drug Sales Analyst, allowed me to do some cross-functional work and collaborate with different departments including Marketing and Product Management teams. This highlights one of the fundamental values of the culture at the company, which is being able to work with the various departments within the company to get experience in various places. The company does a good job of seeing the co-ops/interns in the same eye as other full-time employees. I was given my own office, ID badge, laptop to work from home, etc. just like every other employee. They do not hawk you or feel like you are being treated like a kid; when you are given work, you are expected to get it done timely and with quality, just as every other employee. There is no special treatment for being an intern or held to any different standard than any other full-time employee. My biggest challenge I had during my co-op was the fact that my manager was rarely in the office due to having to travel to his other team member's locations at different company sites. This made it tough to meet with my manager face to face. Adapting to my primary source of communication being phone calls with my supervisor was tough at first, but I learned to deal by developing relationships with other employees and asking them for help on things that need face-to-face answers to. Being a part of the sales team, virtual communication was our basically only source of communication with one another. All of our meetings were done via phone.

Like mentioned prior, my technical role at the company was Food and Drug Sales Analyst. I reported directly to my supervisor, who was in charge of both the West and East Coast sales teams. I was there to provide support to any sales reps on either coasts team. A few computer programs that I used throughout my co-op were Salesforce, Excel, and other proprietary software. This software is allowed for employees to share and collaborate on different content. I did not have day-to-day tasks; all my work was project-based. The bad thing about this was when I was not given a project or something to work on, there was nothing I could really do besides ask around other departments and see if they had any work for me. The days fluctuated with business. There could be a few days up to a week where my manager was traveling and had nothing for me to do and neither did any other departments, so I found myself with a lot of downtime at times. But then there were also days where I came in at 6am and didn't leave until 7pm because of the amount of work I had to get done.

There were a few projects I worked on that I would like to highlight. The first project I want to talk about is actually my first big project. My manager was in charge of the years (2016) United Way campaign while I was there. I started in July, and the campaign kicked off at the end of August. My manager had essentially made the United Way campaign my own project I could be in charge of. We had different events planned throughout the campaign that helped by having people donate money to sign up for the event. For example, one event we had was getting your picture with the Larry O'Brien trophy. The local professional basketball team had just won the championship in June, so everyone was still in celebrating mode and wanted a picture with the trophy. The fee to get your picture taken was $10. You were given a free raffle ticket after paying and were put in a raffle that we selected from at the end of the event. This raffle had smaller prizes in them. However, I was also in charge of the big raffle we had going throughout the entire campaign. For this one, we were raffling off baseball tickets, football tickets, and basketball tickets. Each ticket cost $5 and could buy as many as you wanted. Every 2 weeks we selected winners for a couple games. We also did a drawing at each big event we held throughout the campaign, including the championship trophy event. For each event we had during the campaign, I was the one in charge of basically making sure the event was planned correctly, advertised well and ran smoothly. I kept a running Excel sheet of everyone who bought a ticket, how many tickets, how much they donated, list of each game, winners of each game, and were responsible for actually holding the money.

I worked closely alongside the Coordinator, Community Relations on the campus. This project was outside of my job description. It was a lot of event planning. There were days that my manager would ask me to go down to the cafeteria to advertise and sell raffle tickets during the allotted lunch time (12:00pm-1:00pm) because that's when everyone would be in the cafeteria. I would then take my lunch an hour later, from 1:00pm-2:00pm. Our campaign goal was to raise $10,000 during the 2-month campaign. We exceeded that goal and raised in the $16,000. The raffle I was running during the campaign alone raised 6,000 dollars.

Another project I helped was with our True Value account. I played a vital role in solving financial errors dating back from 2014. I worked closely along with a contractor out in Chicago. Our means of communication was always virtual, via email or phone call. Essentially the project was to update our records within the account and look into any times where our records did not match up with what True Value had in their files. It consisted of me looking through hundreds of Excel sheets, looking for patterns in the data. I was basically the first line of filtration; look through all the data sheets, mark down 'obvious' errors, and highlight those that needed to be checked in more detail. The obvious errors are the ones that the lady from Chicago taught me how to spot. For example, if there is a discrepancy of $100 or so between the company and True Values records, chances are there was a rebate missing. I would then leave a comment in a column I created titled 'Comments' in the spreadsheet saying rebate missing. After going through all hundreds of spreadsheets, I then passed them back along to the contractor to look and do further research where needed. This project was particularly challenging at first because she had to explain everything over the phone relating to Excel that would have been a lot easier and quicker to pick up on if having seen it done in person. Knowing Excel, how to operate it and its different shortcuts were crucial for this project because all my work was done analyzing and manipulating spreadsheets.

The final project I want to go into more detail about was the time I worked with the Product Management Team. There is a funny, well funny now, story relating to this project. The manager of the Product Management Team that I was working with on this project was actually the same lady who took part in my interview for the position. She is a university alumnus and is supposed to help the co-ops from college transition into the role when I first got there and keep in touch with me to see how everything is going. Also, she was supposed to get in contact with me when I accepted the role to give me advice on what to know about the city, good places to live, etc. but never did. No one told me that she was supposed to do this until I found out talking with another co-worker about it. I casually brought up how it was funny I was working on a project with her, and this was the first time we were connecting while I been there because she was one of the people conducting my interview. The co-worker mentioned that how in the past she served as this transition help for college students and gave advice before moving here. I had no clue about this before hearing that. When I met with her, she brought up to me before I even mentioned it how she was sorry we never connected before and how usually she is way more involved with the co-ops. She said it was because she was recently promoted a few weeks before I started, so she had been super busy adapting to the role. She contacted me for the first time in November to help work on this project with her. The project itself was updating 400+ products within our database and then updating the website, taking down old products and putting up the new ones. I was given a massive master spreadsheet with all of the company products and details. I had to go through a list of new products and look up their specific details and update them in a new spreadsheet. When I finished that, I then worked with a lady in charge of practically running the product website. We updated the website with all the new products and replaced the old ones. Again, this project required technical skills in Excel being able to create and manipulate spreadsheets.

One cool thing I was able to do at work, outside of my job description, was to join the African American Forum Club. Headquarters had a bunch of different clubs you were allowed to join while there, just like all the full-time employees. I joined the AAF (African American Forum). We had meetings to discuss different events we were planning on doing, and anyone was able to voice their opinion on anything during meetings. One awesome event we held was a voter registration event. We went to a football game on a Saturday morning at a local high school and had a tent set up where people could come register to vote. We did this in October, right before the election took place. It was nice helping people exercise their right to vote. We went to a high school in the inner city where a lot of the of eligible voters were not registered or cared much to vote. We educated them on the importance of having your voice heard and exercising your right to vote, as it was not too long ago our relatives were not granted these rights. Joining AAF gave me a place to work where I felt I could be 100% myself and feel personally comfortable. I was able to make great connections in the club and developed meaningful relationships.

While I was not given a written evaluation at the end of my co-op, I did have lunch with my manager of my last day where we talked about how I did. He had all positive things to say and let me know that if I ever needed a recommendation of any sort or referral to contact him. I did have one of my co-workers I worked on a few mini projects with writing me a letter of recommendation after my co-op ended.

Regarding how this work experience contributed to my career development, goals and growth, I still feel as that I learned a lot from this experience. While I do not feel completely satisfied with the amount I was able to learn in my field, I feel that I have learned a lot about what to look for and not look for in picking a co-op and then job in the future. I feel that I was able to grow from this experience and become more knowledgeable in what happens within companies. I learned from the different situations I was in and learned what more about myself as a worker and how to interact with others in the workplace. I now know that sales is not my thing and recently picked up that MIS concentration and will be doing my last co-op with a role in marketing automation to try something new.

After doing this last co-op, I knew that I needed to buckle down on my technical skills in Excel and with technology in general, as technology is the future. I am currently taking a Data Mining class as one of my summer classes. I figured having a technical background, being able to manipulate data and analyze it to predict future results, could be crucial in helping expand my options in the future. After doing this co-op, I think Introduction to Computer Science was most helpful. In this class, we learned a lot about the different functions and coding that can be done in Excel. Knowing Excel was a big part of this past co-op; being able to use it and create spreadsheets was necessary.

However, I think that Organizational Behavior was most helpful in my co-op experience. It helped me learn from this past co-op after feeling like I had wasted a co-op because I did not have the time I was expecting to have. In Organizational Behavior, we were taught how to 'play the game.' We learned the ins and outs of organizations. We were taught about the culture of companies and different situations that may occur. It was a class where the discussions were about real-world experience and what to expect after graduation, not just terms and equations we would 95% chance never use again. The terms and theories we learned in this class came during and after talking about our different co-op experiences, basically being like "remember what we were just talking about with your real-life experience? Well, this is what that was called, and this is how you can learn from this, so you are on the winning end of the stick next time."

My experience with the company was actually pretty pleasant. The job paid well, came with nice perks, flexible hours, allowed to work from home occasionally, different events that happen on site. I was able to meet some really nice people who gave me their perspective on life and was able to take away valuable advice. On the flip side, I was not too pleased with my manager actually. I understand that he is busy and had a lot on his plate. However, I do not feel that I was treated right. There would be days that went by that I did not hear from my manager while he was out of the office. Even a couple of my co-workers commented saying how they felt that I was under-used and should have been utilized better. There was a co-op that started in about September. He went to a local college. He was a co-op working in the marketing department. On his first day, he was given three projects. He was brought to speed right away and given a sense of value from the start. He was always busy and being given work. He never felt under-utilized and had a very different, more optimistic view of work then I did because of our two very different situations. I was also disappointed in my transition period to the company. I was not given much sense of direction for things and pretty much had to figure things out on my own. The lady who I mentioned before on the Product Management Team was basically non-existent until my last month where I had things figured out by then. During a meeting I was supposed to have with her, I walked in, and she was on the phone with the new co-op who would be replacing me when I left. She was giving her advice on where to live, things to know, etc. while we were supposed to be meeting. I sat there for about 15 minutes while she answered questions and gave the inside scoop to the new co-op, while she did not even attempt to contact me until my last month there and gave me no direction or feeling of welcome before or at the start of my role.

I would recommend this role for others. I feel that I would have had a much different experience at the company working for a different supervisor then I did. I believe that I would have enjoyed my time and work there a lot more than I did. For others, the co-op could be improved by making sure the manager you are assigning the co-op to actually needs help and is looking forward to working alongside them for six months. Also, there can be a better housing process. In the past, the organization provided housing to all interns/co-ops. Something happened one year where two roommates/co-workers got in a fight, and they switched to just giving a relocation stipend. The allowance is fine, but they could provide some type of housing map describing the different areas and saying where most other co-ops enjoy staying. Other than that, from what I saw and experienced, the company does a great job with their interns/co-ops and have a great leadership program that a lot of past co-ops end up in.

Interviewee #4 of 4

For my first co-op, I worked on the marketing team for a company, which is a mobile payments startup that focuses on the fast-casual restaurant industry. The marketing team focuses on two primary business areas: a B2C focus which relates to the company's own app, and a B2B focus which deals with all of the white label apps that we run. I primarily worked with the white label apps doing marketing analytics for key clients. I worked for the organization full-time for the six months of my co-op and then continued to work for them part-time (3 days a week) while back in classes for five months. When

I first began this co-op, I had just switched to the business school at my university and had not yet decided which concentration I would choose. However, it became evident after a few months at the company that I was not only good at my marketing analytics job but I also actually enjoyed it. After realizing that, I officially declared marketing as a concentration and enrolled in a marketing analytics class.

My position at the company was uniquely important to the overall functioning of the marketing team and the company as a whole. The organization's primary value proposition to the white label clients it works with is that they are able to provide insights on consumer behavior to develop and implement custom marketing campaigns to drive consumer engagement and thus increase revenue. As my job was to use our database of customer transactional and demographic information to extract and present key insights to account managers and clients, I was uniquely positioned to provide the best analytics to clients, improving client relationships for the company. The company hires co-ops because it is an excellent way to find and develop young talent, and they hire many co-ops both full-time and part-time after the program has ended. A significant percentage of the entire company were actually graduates of my university. This particular co-op role is relatively longstanding regarding the company's history. I believe I was part of the fourth or fifth round of co-ops to be hired by the company (keep in mind the company has only existed for five or so years).

When I started at the company, the workforce was tiny (about 80 employees). However, it has been growing rapidly, and I believe total employees numbers now surpasses 150. The structure of the company is relatively siloed in that there are many functional teams (marketing, sales, finance, hardware, etc.), and there is relatively little cross-collaboration, with some exceptions. The company is very much dedicated to providing an exceptional co-op experience. By nature of being a small business, even co-ops had great responsibility and are treated as such. In fact, most people at the company consider me a full-time employee. Within the marketing team, I had a lot of flexibility regarding what projects I wanted to work on and was given a lot of freedom to explore what I was interested in. There was ample opportunity to customize my co-op experience based on what I wanted to get out of it.

As briefly described above, my job was to provide exceptional marketing analytics and consumer insights to key clients. As such, I worked closely with other members of the marketing team as well as account managers to tailor the analytics to precisely match what the client was looking for. As white label clients are the primary revenue driver for the company overall, this was a very important role for me to hold in that I had a direct impact on the value of the company was providing to its clients.

One of the company's marketing team's overall goals is to continually improve our reporting processes for clients. This involves building detailed dashboards that provide key insights into a client's consumer base, campaign performance, overall business statistics, etc. For one specific project, I was tasked with entirely changing the way organization reports on custom campaign performance for clients. The existing dashboard was outdated, too general, and was not providing real value to clients. I conducted research to identify key issues, and challenges clients were having with the dashboard and then redesigned a new dashboard that would address these issues, highlight key insights that were more valuable for clients, and ensure that the dashboard was user-friendly and self-explanatory for clients. I did this by working closely with managers on the marketing team, account managers, and clients. The final product was implemented across 14,000 businesses, and significantly decreased client-reporting requests and freed up marketing time.

On a daily basis, I was responsible for completing client requests for specific reports or for implementing campaigns. Reports required me to develop complex SQL scripts and pull data that would highlight the key insights the client was looking for.

Implementing campaigns required me to design HTML to be sent out via emails, pre-claim credit for specific users, and set up marketing automation systems to actually implement the campaign mechanisms. All of these requests were submitted to a marketing "ticket queue" via the account managers, so I always made sure to monitor the queue and make sure that requests were being completed on time.

For the specific project mentioned in, I went beyond the standard job description by leading client calls to pilot the dashboard before full implementation. Usually, co-ops do not have access to the clients directly, so this was an opportunity for me to expand my job description and experience a more client-facing role. I also took on many other side projects that aimed to improve the overall functioning of the marketing team (e.g., auditing our entire marketing automation system to clear out unnecessary loads on our database, which eliminated delays and issues on campaign executions).

None of the projects and tasks that I worked on involved working with a project team. However, they often involved a lot of collaboration with other team members or other people in the company as specific, technical issues arose. However, these collaborations were usually meant for ad-hoc problem-solving, and I always remained the sole owner of the project.

The responsibilities of my position involved deep knowledge of SQL, HTML, and CSS, as well as getting comfortable with using relational databases, marketing automation software, and communication platforms.

Surprisingly, I never ran into a situation with a project where I needed a specific academic background to complete the project. As mentioned before, I started the job with absolutely no experience in marketing (or even any analytical role) and everything I needed to know I learned on the job. If I needed to do a specific technical function, I just researched how to do it and learned on my own.

As mentioned before, the main project I worked on was aiming to improve reporting processes for custom campaign performance. This was a months-long project and was intended to decrease client's reliance on account managers and the marketing team to supply specific analytics post-campaign. The dashboard was meant to satisfy any potential analytics requests clients might have, decreasing the number of reporting requests put through to the marketing team, freeing up time to spend on other, more valuable tasks.

I used a Redshift database that stored customer's' transactional and demographic information. I used this database to access and visualize customer data that revealed valuable insights for clients. Other software used was business intelligence software used for data visualization, a marketing automation tool, and a tool used to send out both transactional and campaign emails.

My entire position depended on the successful and unique analysis and application of customer data for clients. Clients work with the company to gain unique insights into their customers' behavior to develop more strategic and effective campaigns to influence customer behavior. My job was to provide those insights by analyzing a client's customer data and applying it in a way that was applicable and relevant to serve client needs.

There were no official documents, interviews, or presentations that I was required to complete. However, I drafted project proposals to be approved by a marketing manager, conducted informal interviews with clients to pilot the custom campaign performance dashboard I was building and presented the final dashboard to the account managers to show them how to use it.

As required by the university, my direct manager provided a written evaluation of my co-op experience at the organization. It was overwhelmingly positive and did not contain much critical feedback. This was also true for the weekly one-on-ones I had with my manager throughout my co-op. At the end of the 6-month co-op, I had a meeting with my boss during which he asked if I had any feedback for him regarding the co-op. My response was that I would have appreciated more critical feedback so that I know of areas to improve, as I am always looking to learn and improve.

This was singlehandedly the most valuable experience I have had since arriving at the university concerning career development, goals, and growth. I quite honestly feel like I learned more relevant and useful skills and knowledge during my time at the company than in all of my university courses combined. It solidified my career path and allowed me to set more tangible goals for myself for my next co-op. The experiences I had at the company allowed me to get an amazing second co-op at a company that I would love to work for post-graduation.

After working at the company and realizing I wanted to continue working in marketing analytics as a career, I signed up for an upper-class marketing analytics course for Spring 2017 that turned out to be an extremely valuable class to take. I was able to apply much of what I learned in class to my work at my co-op. A co-worker also recommended I take a digital marketing course, which I am planning on taking during my next semester of classes.

Like I said before when I started this co-op I was a new business major who had not declared any concentration. Previously, I was an International Affairs major and had taken three full semesters of courses within that discipline. None of these courses were remotely applicable to my co-op. The only course I had taken before starting my co-op that was relevant was the Introduction to Marketing course that is required for all business majors. While it was a very general course, it introduced me to the basics of marketing. While it did not delve into strategic marketing techniques or cover any sort of material related to digital marketing, analytics, or campaign-based marketing, it provided a solid foundation so that I had a general idea of marketing terms when I began my co-op.

The most noteworthy distinction between my university education and my on-the-job experience is the level of technical expertise that was developed at the company. Because I switched to marketing after my second year at the university, I did not have the opportunity to add a minor in Computer Science (which, in retrospect, I would have done) and so I do not have the chance to take any technical courses that would benefit me in a data-driven, analytical career. However, throughout my time at this co-op, I reached a level of technical expertise that I do not think could have even been achieved by taking a few classes at the university. I mastered SQL and HTML and got exposure to various business intelligence tools and marketing automation software that set me apart from other applicants in my second co-op search. Personally, I have realized that I learn much better in a real-world situation where I am learning and using a new topic/tool concurrently. My experience prepared me to accept my next co-op position as a Data Analysis and Strategy Operations co-op in the fall, where I will continue to develop my analytical expertise outside of my college education.

As discussed previously, I had no technical background when I began my co-op. However, this type of background was developed throughout my time at the company through extensive work in data analytics and visualization.

My high personal level of satisfaction with this co-op is demonstrated by the fact that I continued to work part-time after my co-op had finished. The opportunities for personal and professional development are endless, and it truly allowed me to explore and find out what I was both interested in and good at professionally. I would absolutely recommend this co-op to others, as it has opened so many doors for me.

As mentioned before, my feedback for my boss regarding how to improve the co-op was that he should try and incorporate more critical feedback for the co-ops throughout their entire time at the company. This would allow co-ops to realize areas for improvement and act upon them continuously, allowing for even more professional development and better overall experience.

CHAPTER 6

MANAGEMENT & CONSULTING

To break into this target-driven industry, you'll need excellent analytical, leadership and organizational skills as well as extensive work experience. Agencies and specialist recruitment websites can be valuable sources of information for identifying vacancies and allow you to keep up to date with key issues in the sector.

You could work either as a general manager or in a specific area such as Marketing, HR or IT. You could also work in consultancy, which involves advising organizations and helping them to solve problems. There is some overlap with the accountancy, banking, and finance sector. Professionals in these industries will often work together to ensure the best outcome for the client.

WHAT DO EMPLOYERS LOOK FOR?

A relevant degree is not necessary but may be advantageous. Depending on their business focus, some employers will seek particular skills such as IT or marketing. A postgraduate qualification, such as an MBA, can help to further your career. The requirements set by smaller companies vary. Many new graduates won't get a consulting or management role immediately after graduation. You'll generally need extensive experience and knowledge of the business world before you can manage a team or offer advice. Employers require typically candidates with: analytical skills and strategic thinking; good interpersonal skills; motivation and leadership skills; organizational and time management skills; and the ability to be flexible and open to change.

HOW DO I FIND A JOB?

Employers in this sector place a strong emphasis on work experience. Many large companies offer summer placements or a year in industry for undergraduate students. These can lead to a permanent job or a place on a graduate scheme. Many large companies are present at university careers fairs, but you can also find details of their schemes—including how to and when to apply—on their websites. A speculative approach is best for smaller companies, so send a resume and cover letter.

WHAT'S THE WORKING CULTURE?

Graduates can expect:

- A high level of responsibility from an early stage, and opportunities for rapid career progression;
- A varied working life, spending time at client sites, away from home and abroad;
- High starting salaries of $55,000 to $70,000 excluding bonuses, rising quickly to around $90,000;
- Self-employment or freelance work to be an option after several years;
- Working hours to be typically long and focused on completing projects to tight deadlines.

CO-OP PARTICIPANT INTERVIEWS

Interviewee #1 of 6

I was employed at a major financial services firm downtown. My duties were two-fold. I had the responsibility of working with the trade support team about half of the day. In this role, I ensured trade settlement as well as ensuring that the share and dollar amounts were correct. The second part of my day was focused on working with the compliance team. In this role, I ensured that the "Know Your Client" documentation was correct. I also helped with year-end reviews of clients ensuring that all information was up to date. During this role, I also began to manage a team in India. They were responsible for a lot of the day-to-day work, while my original team and I focused on the larger deliverables.

The work experience was tough and trying. I initially only accepted the trade support role, without the knowledge that I would be asked to assist another team. The addition of these responsibilities meant that I was working long hours while also managing the expectations and deadlines of both teams I was working on.

The position's contract was for six months, and initially with the trade support team. My role was to check incoming wires and withdrawals, to ensure that the share and dollar amounts were correct, as well as that all the information that was required was correct as well. There was supposed to be some large project-oriented work as well, but to my dismay, it had already been completed in advance of my start date. The position was my first co-op, so I had not taken that many specialized classes, but I had previous work experience in the financial community.

My position's value to the company was unclear. It was important in the sense that we had to ensure that the clients we had received the correct amount of funds at the appropriate time, as these were major institutional clients who needed the funds promptly. It was clear that my role was needed to ensure that the firm functioned on a day-to-day level. However, due to the nature of the situation within the firm at the time, I ended up helping out in areas that I had not expected. The projects I worked on for the compliance team were extremely important, so much so that senior management assigned us a project manager who reported to people very high up on the command chain. The firm is one of my university's largest co-op partners and has had co-ops for many years. They hire co-ops not only to scout for future talent, as several past co-ops have been invited to their rotational and development programs but also because they need labor to help them complete projects as well as to do day-to-day functions. Co-ops are not paid as much as full-time employees, so it makes sense for them to seek out motivated students to fill short-term needs for the firm.

I was working at the firm during the rollout of the major initiative as they called it, as well as the push to motivate the compliance team to be the first line of defense for the company. It has been some time since I worked there, so I cannot recall specifics and do not have access to the internal documents. There was a strong emphasis on personal and team accountability, as errors were tracked as well as discussed to evolve the methods used by the firm.

The firm employs about 40,000 employees and about 120 co-ops, both within the US and abroad. The firm had three main silos of operations, the bank, and trust company (global services), global advisors, and global markets. The firm was committed to its co-ops offering lecture series as well as the opportunity to communicate with both previous co-ops now employed at the firm, as well as upper-level employees who could act as mentors. However, due to the size of the firm, as well as my role, it was difficult at times to access these options within the firm. I found that students who worked at smaller firms, or who worked on smaller teams, had a more involved co-op experience, as they were able to leverage their contributions on a more effective level.

The positions I held were both part of teams overseen by a function manager who reported to a vice president. Both roles were important as they contributed to the ability of the firm to function on a day-to-day level, as well as ensure that the firm was in compliance going forward. The work I was doing was important to the company, as it served their clients' needs, as well as the firm's.

The trade support team had one main goal, to ensure that all transactions were completed in the correct manner, as well as with the correct party. The high volume of work ensured that every day was a challenge, but the technology on hand made it difficult at times. It took a while for me to be given the licenses to use the relevant products, which unfortunately made it difficult to contribute right away. The compliance team had many various goals. From serving as the first line of defense to prevent both money laundering as well as ensuring that the firm itself only did business with reputable counterparties. There were several large projects, which I worked on with the compliance team. The volume of work for these projects, however, was immense, something that was compounded by a lack of manpower. Also since only some of the employees had access to the relevant technology, the process was hampered in its effectiveness.

My duties were two-fold for this co-op. I had the responsibility of ensuring trades were booked correctly with the correct amounts of shares and dollars. For the compliance part of my duties, I had several functions. I was responsible for evaluating authorized signors as politically exposed persons. This process led to me conducting a cursory background check on certain people to ensure that they had not committed major financial crimes as well as make sure that they did not have felonies on their records. I was also responsible for conducting reviews of entire clients to ensure that they had submitted proper documentation, as well as ensure that they had provided entirely correct information. During my duties here, I had begun to manage a team based in India, where they assisted with the politically exposed people searches. This was due to the limited manpower, as well as a limited license for certain products that we used. I had to review all of this team's work, as well as ensure that they understood the methods that were being used and the logic behind the evaluation process.

I was recruited as a client-trading associate, whereby my entire job was supposed to be with the trade support team. However, midway through I was asked to assist on a compliance project, and eventually, that project and compliance work became my job.

I actively participated in projects. Our year-end review of compliance materials as well as of clients was of such importance that a direct project manager had been appointed by upper-level management to ensure that the project was brought to fruition on time. This led to me communicating across many areas of the firm, which made for an interesting learning experience.

The specific technical functions of this position were rather limited. The only real technical requirement was to be able to use the software provided to complete your task. I was not writing macros or using Excel as much as I expected.

To be honest, the project and work that I did didn't draw on any academic background. I found myself not really applying what I had learned in school, possibly because the role I was moved to was not what I had applied to do. Most of the knowledge that I picked up during my time, there was learned on the job, or by approaching a manager or employee to ask to talk about the issue.

The goals of the project that I worked on were to meet the deadlines. While goals were tracked, such as the completion of individual tasks such has my examination of the politically exposed persons; the overall project was driven by a submission deadline for the documents from the firm. Abstractly one could say that the goal was to ensure that all clients and their board members had been properly vetted to ensure that the firm was not complicit in any money laundering or potentially engaging with counterparties who were under sanctions.

The key data we looked for in the compliance area of my job were convictions for major felonies or ties to terrorist organizations. We used a proprietary software tool, and if we were still unable to match the person on the company's board/authorized signor, or there was further due diligence required we would use Lexus Nexus for a more detailed examination of the individual. For the trade support role, I had to predominately keep my eye on the account #, the dollar amount on the faxed ticket, and the denomination of the currency

I did not operate any machinery in the role except for the occasional fax. These would be NIGO (not in good order) trades that we faxed back because they were missing critical information, or the data received did not match up with what was received through the portal.

I was required to take the data retrieved and analyze it against whatever we could find on the individual. This included searching middle names, the area of residence as well as if they were related to any individuals who worked in politics. This data was then used to discount or confirm hits we received on these individuals. Any matches were escalated to CRM's to ensure that the individual was in good standing as well as making sure that a full background check was run.

Besides a report template that showed any matches as well as filling out the required fields on the template (company name, ID number, etc.) I did not put together any reports or presentations.

The assessment of my work was exceedingly high. I had made sure that despite the circumstances of my time and being thrown into a new role, I understood what I was doing and attempted to lead as much as possible. I created a sort of process bible for several individual processes as well as for larger projects in the future.

What I learned most from this experience was how to operate in a corporate environment. I also learned what I did not want to do as a future career. I figured out that I did not want to work in compliance or in a role where I was not privy to the investment decisions. I also came away with a sense of how to ask for what I want, especially with regards to exposure to materials. Since I personally was moved to a role that I had not applied to or had interest in, I had to go through other channels of communication to gain the exposure that I wanted. Due to the team's project I worked on, I also learned how to communicate with a project manager appointed by high-level management.

With regards to my future coursework, this co-op did not really shine a light on any area. I only had minimal exposure in the end to what I had wanted. I did not change my coursework decision because of this co-op. On my second co-op, however, I did take recommendations from several investment team members as well as co-workers as to what I should focus on and how to improve myself.

That this role did not draw on any coursework, something that I was rather upset about. Instead, I pulled the values of perseverance and diligent hard work that I had learned throughout my scholastic career.

The significant differences between my on-the-job and in-class experience were the subject matter I was dealing with. I had no exposure to the compliance area. I also realized that I am someone who is more driven when I can really sink my teeth into analytical

111

work, rather than day-to-day task work. I also found the difference between a work mentor and an academic mentor. Scholastic mentors at that point in my life had been merely for a deeper understanding of issues I found interesting as well as examining topics that were only covered briefly that I wished to expand my exposure too. I had thought of a workplace mentor as someone who was able to advocate for you but only expose you to new stuff at his or her discretion. I came away from this co-op with a good understanding of how to marry these two types of mentorship, especially about future career options as well as to explore new topics.

I felt that this co-op did not make good use of my technical background. I had taken Microsoft Excel Courses, as well as a financial management course, neither of which was really used during this co-op experience. I think that the switching of my role was a major reason for this, as instead of working with a more financial team, I was instead sent to work on a compliance team.

I was unsatisfied with this co-op. Initially, it was because I was switched off of the role which I applied for, but it soon came to be that I was not interested in the work assigned. I also felt that the initial position I was given was not what I was told it would be in the interview. The lack of technical information that the role drew on was also something that I felt disappointed about since I was not able to meet my learning objectives for the co-op. (It may serve you well to speak to a co-op coordinator about the reflections that co-op students must do during and after their co-op.) I would not recommend the compliance co-op. For the trade support co-op, I believe that one must ensure that it is an area that they want to go into before accepting it. I personally did not enjoy it, but I know others have.

I think that the co-op could have been improved by making sure that there was time away from the day-to-day activities to learn more. I had almost no opportunity to meet with others and learn more about the industry or specific areas due to the large volume of work. I found that since it was such a large firm, the co-ops could be viewed as expendable since they have a new class coming in relatively quickly. Yes, certain co-op employees are offered to return, or take on more advanced roles, but it is rare at large firms compared to smaller firms.

Interviewee #2 of 6

My first co-op was at a New England insurance company. I worked as a Business Analyst (BA) within the IT department. I worked at the company for six months. During my time there, I performed many duties such as writing and executing test cases for new upgrades being released each month, collaborated with another co-op student to develop a company-specific business glossary, and worked extensively on Excel to sort and identify policies that could be used during the testing phases of a project. When I was searching for co-ops, I had actually been focused on looking for consulting and HR experiences. One day I met with my advisor, and she told me about this opportunity, so I decided to give it a chance and interview. When I was offered the job, I accepted because even though it wasn't in the exact field that I had been targeting in my search, I knew I would learn a lot through the job responsibilities and the company. It was also an excellent opportunity to experience an office culture and figure out what I like and don't like about that working environment.

Before starting the co-op, I had no idea what a BA did within an insurance company (or any company for that matter). However, I quickly realized just how valuable each BA is to the company because mostly, they are the link between the developers and the business. Whenever the business wants a new upgrade that will help to better serve both internal and external customers, it is a BA's job to make sure they understand what exactly needs to be done and then communicate those needs to the developers who will actually create the services, like upgraded websites. A business analyst makes sure there is a constant and transparent dialogue between both parties for the duration of the project. Even as a co-op, I was able to attend meetings and have a real impact on projects I was assigned to through work that I was given. I was also trained on how to use company-specific systems so that when data needed to be identified for testing and when testing actually had to happen, I was able to step up and be a contributing member of the team. Past co-ops have proven to the company that students of my university are observant and quickly able to learn new systems and pick up the knowledge needed to actually assist on teams. Whenever someone found out I was a co-op, they always had praise and excellent comments about previous co-ops that they had worked with. Something that I realized was extremely valued by the company was the fact that co-ops were usually able to grasp new concepts and software quickly but also comfortably. In a fast-paced environment with constantly moving parts, it's important to be able to quickly train a co-op but also have them understand so that they are able to figure out questions on their own. Of course, everyone was always open to questions if you had any. The company has had co-ops for a few years now, but I am not sure how many. It is definitely not a new program for them at this stage.

The company mission statement captures what the company provides to each policyholder, which is constant support in times of need. The company serves policyholders in New England and with this smaller reach (as opposed to a nationwide company), they are able to understand each state's specific needs and tailor their services to provide the most comprehensive service that they can. For employees, one award that is emphasized is that the company has been named 'best places to work' for nine consecutive years in the extra-large business category. This award gives you an idea of the kind of culture that is present at the company. The company takes care of their employees through lunches, events like Customer Service Appreciation Week, opportunities to win tickets to different sporting/ entertainment events, among many other events. And even as a co-op, I was always able and encouraged to take part in events. During my time, I volunteered three times, attended a few lunches they hosted, and participated in a 'cup-stacking' competition event with the other co-ops during Customer Service Appreciation Week.

Within the Headquarters, I would describe the structure as functional, with different departments organized by duties. For example, while I worked in the IT department, there was also a corporate communications department, auditing, finance, etc. During my co-op cycle, there were two co-ops in the IT department, and also one in internal auditing, and one in finance. The company is committed to providing college students searching for co-ops with multiple positions to which they can apply to and gain exposure in that field. Once at the company, there are workshops (like Business Writing, How Insurance Works, and Listening to Build Relationships), job shadows in different departments, volunteer opportunities, and the opportunity to get your yellow belt Six Sigma Certification. While on co-op, I took part in all the before mentioned opportunities. Each co-op is also assigned not only a manager but a mentor as well, and you meet with each respectively weekly or bi-weekly, depending on everyone's schedules.

Although my position was not critical in the sense that if I did not show up for work one day, everything would stop, I did come to realize how my individual work was contributing to my team which in turn contributed to the overall organization. I was never given a task that was menial or what I would consider busy-work. My team relied on me to get my responsibilities done because that allowed them to keep on track with their own work. When they were on track with their work, it meant that the developers were able to work on the new upgrades. This led to projects being completed that the business wanted and in turn led to internal and external users having even better interactions with company systems.

The key goal of each upgrade I was a part of was to make the website/system more user-friendly and easy to understand. For example, I worked on one project that was the improvement of the CRM website that internal customers used to assist policyholders when they called in with questions. Even though I had not seen the previous interface, anytime someone who used the site knew I was working on the upgrade, they were so excited that changes were going to be made and that it was going to be easier to understand. For this project, I was specifically in charge of executing test cases that others had written which documented what was supposed to happen when different links on the screen were clicked and/or information was put into the system. I also recorded any defects I came across. I think the primary challenge that each project faced was fewer resources than would have been ideal. For example, I was not originally on the CRM project but was pulled in along with another co-op to help test during the final stages of the project because they needed more testers. With everyone being allocated to working on multiple projects at one time, it was understandably difficult to be fully dedicated to one project, which led to some challenges when it came to testing.

Duties

Depending on the project assigned, my day-to-day responsibilities and activities varied. A typical day would start with me checking emails and responding to any that had come in before I had arrived to work. From there, I would attend any meetings I had in the morning. If I didn't have meetings, I would begin working on my designated work for a project. For example, when I first started, I spent a lot of time on Excel sorting through policies and identifying ones that could be used when it came to the testing stage of the project. Around month 4, I learned how to read and execute a test case and would spend a good portion of my day executing those test cases. When I learned how to write test cases, I would divide up my day between writing and executing. When I was working on the glossary project, I would also allocate a few hours of my day to filter and clean the spreadsheet by removing duplicate terms and finding missing definitions for ones that were missing. Throughout my workday, I would also check-in with whoever had assigned me to work whenever I had questions, or I had finished my work.

Admittedly, I spent my first few months so focused on doing a good job with the work that I was assigned that I never looked to taking on duties beyond the standard job description. When I started to feel more comfortable and confident, I did find that although it was still within the job description, I was looking to take on more projects at once to not only learn more about the different types of projects BA's work on but also to learn how to manage my time because I know once I graduate, it will be an important skill to have for any job. When I was reaching a point of not knowing how to allocate my time to meet all my demands, I was grateful to be able to speak with my manager and others on my teams for guidance. Juggling multiple projects at once is nothing new, so being able to gain some insight from those who have gone through and continue to deal with this workplace challenge was extremely valuable.

The specific team I was on was the Project Management Office for the IT department, so my team was rarely working on the same project at the same time. The project managers were individually in charge of their own respective teams, and I only began working on their teams later on. Once on their teams, a lot of my work dealt with testing, and I had to coordinate my findings with members of my team so that if a defect showed up, it could be fixed in time before a release. There was a lot of coordination between my co-workers and me because I had to be able to communicate to them, but they also had to keep me in the loop if something was actually supposed to be working a certain way that was different from what was written in the test cases, etc.

Some examples of technical functions of my position included extensive work with Excel and also company-specific systems. The function of my role concerning using these systems/ programs involved manipulation of data and data sorting, usually as part of the beginning stages of a project's lifecycle.

To be successful on any project I worked on, I needed to be able to use Word and Excel comfortably, both of which I learned to use in school. Concerning actual business courses that I had taken before co-op, there was not really any class that I can say I needed to have taken to be able to do my work. I had taken financial accounting, marketing, financial management, international business, calculus, and intro to writing before co-op. Of all those classes, I would say writing helped me the most because I was equipped with tricks and techniques on how to make my messages clearer in emails and documents that I wrote. That being said, it was important to have taken the classes that I did because each gave me introductions to working on new teams with business-focused outcomes, and I believe that was helpful to me when it was actually time for me to work on a real business team. I didn't have any prior insurance knowledge before starting, but through the classes, I took at the company and just being exposed to constant insurance terminology and information, I was able to pick up the information I needed to understand and do my work.

The overarching goal of every project I worked on was to improve the user experience. Breaking it down a bit more, the goal of the CRM project was to make internal users interactions with customers more pleasant. The goal of the Commercial Auto upgrade was to provide underwriters with a more user-friendly website. Even the glossary was aimed at bringing all useful terms into one easy-to-access database for internal users.

On Excel, key data that I generated was filtering and showing how many terms, we had (for the glossary) in different categories like policy-related terms. I used functions and equations such as pivot tables, v-lookups, and simple creations of filters to sort data. I also worked a lot with systems that are specific to the company. These systems are used to access policies, and when I started, I was trained on how to use the systems to find auto policies. On one system, I learned how to find policies, understand the information that was being shown on the screen, and then later I learned how to even enter new policies into the system that could be processed and used for testing later on.

When I was working on the glossary project, I worked with another co-op to figure out how much data (terms) we had, how many were duplicates, and what potential categories within insurance they could fall into. When we created our pivot table that showed what data was policy-related etc. we had to analyze what that data actually showed. We looked for categories that needed more terms, and when we met with the project leaders, we were able to show them what categories were still lacking in some respects. Even though the pivot tables were not going to be shown to people when they went into the glossary, it was important to understand the type of information we had already collected to continue building a more comprehensive glossary.

I completed one presentation at the end of my co-op that was a summary of my learning goals going into the co-op, my overall experience, projects I worked on, and my lessons learned. This was presented to managers, mentors, and representatives from HR during my last week at the company. I completed numerous test case documents where I wrote out what a tester needed to see when they were testing a system. I also completed Excel sheets known as 'Rate Tools' where I would input the data about a policy and at the end; it would provide me the premium amount. I would then compare the premium from the Rate Tool with the one on another system to verify whether or not they matched.

Through verbal and written feedback, I was told that my work was consistently done to a clear and high standard, with very few errors. Some constructive feedback I received dealt mostly in the area of time management skills, especially when I first learning how best to juggle multiple projects at once. In the evaluation my manager wrote for me at the end, she explained that I at first struggled with time allocation but was able to figure out a process that worked best for me. When I first started and was working on sorting and identifying policies on Excel, my co-workers showed me better ways to display the data so that it was clear and easy to understand. Through all the feedback I was given, I was able to structure my finished work in straightforward formats.

I left my co-op more confident and willing to take risks than when I had started. I learned to not be afraid to make mistakes and ask questions, which has already proven valuable when I returned to classes because I spoke up more in my classes and challenged myself. And I know when I start my next co-op soon that I am already in a more confident mental state than I was when I began my first co-op. My co-op at the company has helped me shape my career goals in the sense that I now know what I want to get emotionally from a job. Even though I still don't know yet what exactly I want to build a career in, I have seen the true difference it makes to actually enjoy your job and the people you work with. This co-op has helped me see the value in researching and learning as much as possible about any future jobs because I know not everywhere I go will be as open and warm a culture as this company. I am now open to the idea of becoming a BA, and through my experience, I have seen what sorts of skills are essential to succeeding in the role. If I do become a BA, I have a clearer sense of what I need to learn and improve on to be successful not only as an insurance company BA but elsewhere as well.

My work experience helped me to solidify my choice as a Management concentration student because even though managing people is something you learn with each new team, I understand the importance of taking courses that will help me build the foundational skills I would need as a manager or leader. I am also looking for more opportunities to take courses that work heavily in Excel because even though I worked on Excel a lot during my co-op, there is always room to learn even more. Most of the courses I have left to take in my college career are the fundamental classes that all business students take but with the electives I have left, I am looking to take writing-intensive courses as well to develop my writing skills.

I took a basic Excel and Access course at my university before starting a co-op, and I am glad I did because it put me on a stronger starting point when it came to using Excel comfortably at work. Key principles learned were basic and advanced Excel functions (filtering, pivot tables, macros, v- and h- lookups) and queries on Access. I also felt that the writing course I took freshman year prepared with me with basic writing skills that allowed me to be more effective on the job. Many of my courses had group projects, which prepared me with skills that I could apply to my team concerning communication and keeping everyone on target to completing a project. I think the least applicable course for me was calculus just because I never needed to know any of the formulas/ concepts I had learned during that course.

Bringing up time management again, I found that this area really provided me with the most noteworthy distinction between education/ classes and on- the- job experience. Before starting a co-op, I thought I had a pretty good grasp on my time management skills and had even claimed it during interviews as a strength. What I realized was that in college, as long as I got the work done on time and well, I could choose whenever I wanted to do the work, whether it was over the weekend, late one afternoon, or early in the morning. Once I started work, I quickly saw that even though I had an almost 8-hour work day, I was juggling different responsibilities at once during that allotted time. Once I left for the day and over the weekend, I couldn't do work because I did not have a company laptop. Realizing that distinction between time management in different settings really helped me put into perspective just one of the areas in which college and on-the-job vary.

This co-op made good use of my Excel technical background because I had to be comfortable using it and learning new and efficient ways to manipulate data. I was also given work using formulas that I hadn't used before, and that was a great way for me to take the initiative and learn new ways of using Excel.

Looking back on my co-op experience, I am grateful and happy that I took a chance on a field and career that I had not even thought about during my initial job search. As a first co-op (and even for second and third co-ops) I truly believe that the company provides students with real-world experience along with the guidance needed to make the most of the experience. The classes and workshops tailored specifically to co-ops helped allow us to get to know each other even though we were working in different departments and also exposed us to new aspects of insurance that we did not know about. I would highly recommend both the co-op position and company to other students, and I would also say that even if you haven't thought about being a BA before, give it a chance because you learn a lot that can be applied to any role in the future.

My area of improvement is directed directly toward the BA position, as I did not have much experience with the other positions. Before starting, I had done research into what a BA does but still wasn't too sure exactly what my role would be. I think that with this being a position that is so critical, it would have been beneficial to have a clearer understanding of both the impact of my role and also projects I would be working on at the start of the co-op, maybe as part of a co-op orientation. During my first few months, I was unsure of how my work was having an impact, so I think providing this clarification early on provides new co-ops with a better understanding of what their role is going to be over the course of the six months.

Interviewee #3 of 6

I did my first co-op for discount clothing retailer where I worked as a compensation analyst. The job required me to provide with detailed compensation recommendation for new hires and newly promoted employees. I was also conducting a lot of market research to make sure that the company's compensation structure aligned well externally. The company did not allow co-ops to work more than 40 hours a week and I worked 40 hours most weeks but had to stay in late sometimes depending on the workload.

Compensation was very valuable in recruiting good talent and keeping it. That is the reason that the company paid great attention to its compensation team. While I was there, we did not have, many issues regarding employees raising concerns about their compensation that proved that the company was doing a good job with their compensation. The company has had a longstanding relationship with my university and generally hires around 30 co-ops for their two offices. This has helped them recruit college students fresh out of college, and that was something that they stressed on while I was there as well. They want to build long-lasting relationships with their co-ops as that helps them recruit students with prior knowledge of their business model.

The company hires around 2000 employees, so they are a fairly big company. They try very hard to integrate co-ops into their regular work and provide numerous opportunities to shadow other departments to further learn about their business. There is hierarchical work structure in place at the company but the company culture is extremely welcoming, and everyone is willing to help. I did more work for other people in my department than I did for my direct manager

My job required me to provide compensation analysis for newly promoted or hired associates. I first sent my analysis over to senior members of the team who approved it before I could send it over to HR business partners. Either the compensation was accepted by the new associate, or they came back with the desired compensation. The senior members of my team would then look at the situation and communicate with the HR business partner accordingly. I felt valued and important while working at the company because my team relied heavily on me when they required these analyzes and I felt that I did my best to make sure that no associate was paid unfairly at the company.

Beside these day-to-day analyzes, I was also given the responsibility to conduct market research for compensation and compare that with the compensation structure for an international company. This international company was newly acquired by the company, and our AVP was traveling a week before my end date. In my last couple of months, I was heavily invested in this project, and this was a big challenge as it was hard to find job matches for the jobs that Trade Secret had and was quite a big project to tackle. This required me to communicate with my team members regularly, and I was also communicating with the international office and was in touch with our AVP once she visited the country.

My activity consisted of providing compensation analyzes for the associates. On average, I would get about 10 to 15 of these in a day. The volume of these would vary as I was doing a lot more of these before the company declared their annual bonuses and salary increases. Besides this, I would be assigned projects that kept me busy.

Some of the projects that I was assigned were conducting market research to see whether fulfillment center associates are paid more than distribution center associates or not. I found out that nationally there was not a difference between the compensation of these two departments. I presented this to our AVPs and SVP that made it a great learning experience. Another project that I participated in was evaluating the compensation structure for the distribution center associates to align them with our corporate associates.

Almost everything I did required coordination with other members of my team. All my projects were in collaboration with a member of the team, and it depended on whose department it concerned. I had my team members as guides to make sure that I was moving in the right direction. I showed my projects to the concerned team member before presenting it to the AVP or the SVP. Someone on the team also approved my compensation analysis before being sent out.

The job required a good knowledge of Excel, PowerPoint, and Oracle. I spent a lot of my time on Excel and had to do functions like lookup tables, charts, etc. I would not say that my job was very technical because in compensation there are always some exception or the other because you are dealing with individuals. I felt that it was more of common sense as opposed to technical skills.

The most important class that I took before starting this co-op was a computer science class. This taught me Excel which was very important at work and was also very important in helping me get this co-op. Besides that, it was all mostly common sense, and I guess your math had to be decent and there was attention to detail required for the job as there were always cases of exceptions when dealing with people's compensation.

The goals of all project that I was involved in was to make sure that all employees were paid fairly. As our SVP used to say that no employee would ever tell you that they are overpaid, but our job was to make sure that they did not feel underpaid. This was my goal when completing all my projects.

The main analysis that I did was looking at market data on compensation. Many different surveys were used in this analysis, and I could use different surveys to prove a point when it was required. Also, we had every employee's data on Oracle, and from there we could export data to Excel for particular employees when needed. This data was further used when providing a compensation analysis for new employees and newly promoted employees.

I was required to set up a one-on-one meeting with everyone on my team within my first couple of weeks at the company. Besides this, my manager always encouraged me to set up meetings with as many people as I liked to get to know the business better. Since I did not receive any formal training, I got to know my work in these meetings. I did three presentations when working at the company. All these were different analysis and were presented to the AVP and SVP. All my individual compensation analysis for individual employees was called side by side. These included my salary recommendation for the employee along with their bonuses and the projected payout for the employee for the next three years. They also included the compensation analysis for other employees in the same job.

I was given a written evaluation from my manager, and he had great things to say about me. I showed my evaluation to my interviewers for my next co-op, and they were immensely impressed, and I believe it played a vital role in helping me get the co-op. My manager was very impressed with the speed that I worked and the quality of my work. She said that she would love to write me any recommendations, but for now, I did not need one.

It was a great experience as I got to work in an office and learned how to work in teams and how to conduct myself in an office environment. I'm glad that I worked at the company for my first co-op because of the very friendly work environment. It would be a great stepping stone as I'm moving to financial services for my next co-op. For career goals, I don't think it contributed much because I don't want to work in compensation again as I found it very monotonous. To be honest, I don't think any other business class helped me much. Most of the work was common sense.

I feel that there is a lot more free time when I'm in class, and I can schedule my day to my convenience. In co-op, I felt that I had very little free time and I could not schedule my day to my convenience. Co-op also gets very monotonous with time as opposed to classes.

I did not get to use the technical skills that I developed in classes during my co-op. I think anyone could have done well on this co-op as long as they thought rationally.

I would say that I'm happy with my first co-op because I was given responsibility to do relevant work. I have heard stories about other first co-op experiences where people were idle all day and hated it. The company is also well respected among employers, and I noticed that people reacted very positively when I told them that I did my first co-op at the company.

They have had co-op working in this department for very long. They have a very good idea of what they require from their co-ops. I think that they have a very good hang of how to treat their co-ops and I can't really think of many improvements that they can make.

Interviewee #4 of 6

I currently work a property management company in the city. Our management office is located in the city. I am finishing up my fifth month of a six-month co-op in their headquarters office. This position in property management fits into all facets of financial knowledge, management knowledge (people and buildings), as well as give me a glance into the legal aspects involved in condominiums, and individual landlords. Client relationship management is another responsibility I am strengthening here as well.

The value of my position, Assistant Property Manager, was to come on and help the director of operations with business operation improvements, as well as help out full-time property managers with their extensive portfolios. The company hired a co-op because the newly hired director of operations knew the value of the university co-op program. The plan is his mind was to establish a program that would act as a pipeline for employees in the future. I was the first ever co-op here.

Two statements are always read at the beginning of our bi-weekly manager's meetings, our mission statement, and our company goal.

The commitment to the co-op program of the company is still immature, only time will tell if it can survive. There is, unfortunately, less and less interest in this aspect of the real estate industry, so having the position is one thing, but filling it is another. The company is currently less than 50 employees. The company's structure consists of a few different departments. There is the president, two assistant vice presidents, and the director of operations that are considered the executive team. Under the assistant vice presidents are four full-time property managers, two senior property managers, and a regional property manager. Under the property managers are the assistant property managers and the co-op. Under the director of operations is an accounting department of five employees and a front office employee who manages all day-to-day tasks. Along with this management team for properties, we also have an in-house maintenance team. Our facilities director manages that team, and he coordinates between eight to ten guys.

My role fits into the company in a couple of different ways. I was involved in the general assisting in other property managers with capital projects and budgeting, but that was only one part. Being brought on by the director of operations, I was placed with him to help with developing new organizational strategies and business process improvements. I really got to wear every hat in the organization. When I first came in, my supervisor obviously didn't have any experience with me, so he was cautious about the projects he gave me. When I started finishing my projects a lot earlier than he had anticipated, he wasn't able to keep me busy all the time. So, I started just pushing into what others did on a daily basis. I was just there, watching and listening.

In just about any business, the company is looking for the highest efficiency in processes with the lowest cost to the organization. Some goals of the company are to retain employees in a business with a high employee turnover rate. One project I was working on was developing a property report for each property. When you have over 280 associations and about 35 apartment buildings; which all totals to around 4,500 units, forgetting a specific trait about a specific property is nearly impossible if not written down. Developing this tool would work for the organization is a couple of ways. It would help with manager's answering specific questions to trustees who may be testing them, and it also could help if we had an employee leave they could easily just read these sheets and have something to work with. Another project I was involved in was making property report cards, which rolled into portfolio report cards, and into an organization report card.

My day was never the same. In this business market, you can never know what exactly you'll be doing that day. One thing that is concrete with daily responsibilities is checking your email. Besides that, I was given the ability to work on many different projects, leaving my activities planned out by me either the day of or the day before.

The job description I signed during onboarding really just outlined a job that was geared toward assisting others with their projects. When first started, I stayed in those boundaries. After people started figuring out I could handle a lot more, I started taking the lead, instead of actually assisting. In some cases, I had the property manager assisting me.

I was either part of the organization improvement team which myself and director of operations worked together on, or I would work as a team with the property manager, a contractor and the trustees. The biggest technical trait you need is organization, and I thought I was before taking the co-op, but I have learned a lot more since starting.

For small capital projects, you really only need to have a basic knowledge of construction. In high school, I used to work on the weekends and my summers working for a construction company. I also own a landscape construction company now, so I have a decent technical background, though I'm always looking to learn more. When it comes to the business process improvements, it felt like I was doing work an MBA graduate might do. I was mapping out processes, developing reports on each process, as well as other processes involved, and then mapping out those processes. As of today, we have taken many "liquid" processes and "frozen" them in a state that is repeated daily. This organizational change was difficult to implement at first, but after we communicated how we are here to improve everyone's work life, they started to buy in.

The goals of most projects are to figure out the best solution to a problem. Most projects we work on are engineered capital projects so as property managers you need to be the manager of it all. In regards to some of my business improvement projects, my main goal was to find a way to mitigate total change to the process, while achieving maximum efficiency throughout.

The main software I used was both our proprietary management software and Excel. Other key data generated was from either speaking with property managers or sometimes I would jump into our accounting system and try to dig information out of there.

I had a few business improvement projects, but I will use the first one, the entire maintenance division/work order process re-vamp project. Analyzing the data was the fun part. A lot of people would like to chime in with their opinions and offer what they think would fix the issue. Not to name anyone but a few people told me to "do it this way." I would have agreed with their thought process but would say, "let's get the data first." They would look at me like I had just disrespected them, but when the data came together, I would show them they were either right or wrong. A couple of times I was able to show when the real data came in, the numbers would show that a particular problem of money loss or inefficiencies didn't come from the obvious place and that where it actually did come from had a minor fix.

I was required to write up reports of my findings and then present it to the president of the company. Writing the reports had a learning curve involved. The first report for the first project has more pen ink than printer ink on it, which I plan to keep forever by the way.

My 30-day review went very well, but I know my final assessment will better. To me, working is just another thing to me. I believe you don't start you won't finish, and when you start you make sure you give it your all. The most common compliment I got was on my work ethic and ability to adapt, and working with others.

As I am young and I am absorbing everything which I use in some way or another to help in my career and growth overall, I believe I gained a large amount of experience, contacts, and overall growth to not only my career but to me personally. I learned not only how to run a business, but how not too as well. That can be said about property managers that I would work with. I used to go around and ask how I could help if it were slow during the week, and by the third month, I knew what manager to avoid completely. She taught me a valuable lesson believe it not: how to deal with difficult people in an office.

I believe in the influence of certifications and licenses, I have 3 professional licenses already and two in the works to be completed by the end of this year. Being in this business, many certifications can help you be a better you. I know those have now been put on my radar working with others who have them, so that is in my future coursework. In regards to college coursework, I have planned ahead to take some very interesting ones that I knew about before this co-op. Also, my university doesn't offer many Real Estate related courses.

I'd say some of the most important classes I took were during the semester after my first co-op. I came back from working full-time; I was fresh, rested and ready to be engaged on an academic level. I feel like I made the most of those classes, and was able to relate a 6-

month experience to it. I've been working my whole life; after school, on the weekends, while also playing sports. But going on co-op allowed me to make a job the main priority, I didn't have to revolve it around school. It was a great experience and felt good to come back into classes that fall semester after.

There are huge distinctions between on-the-job experience and education classes. Since I enjoy working, I enjoy co-op. One major obstacle I have to overcome is maintaining a disciplined, healthy schedule. On co-op, you are required to work during a specific timeframe. Back on campus, you're required to be in class, but where you go in between them is up to you. You have to maintain that discipline to not slack off.

This co-op definitely allowed me to bring my technical skills to the forefront. My landscape construction business specializes in Hardscapes. One of the property managers found this out and told me to take care of a project at one of his buildings involving a hardscape. I was able to get the lowest bid while maintaining a great look and maximize warranties because I know the industry and knew what they should use. I was also able to bring my observation skills to the job as well. I developed an inspection report that not only helps managers stay ahead with their buildings; it also generates a ton of work for the maintenance division. When I was field testing this report, I was able to show my technical skills and knowledge in building systems and building infrastructure.

I was definitely satisfied with this co-op. I met a lot of good people and a couple of not so great. But to me, that is the beauty of life and learning. I would recommend this co-op to other students. I wish more students would be interested in this side of real estate.

I would not want the co-op to be "improved for others." I want this organization to be the best of the best, but I would want any student accepting the position here to come in and see how to make something the best.

Interviewee #5 of 6

My first co-op I had the pleasure of working with the Global Procurement Team at a major management consulting firm. I worked there for a total of seven months, considering they requested that I started a week early for training, and we extended my internship by three weeks at the end of the internship. Regarding the academic timeline: this internship happened my first semester of junior year, essentially replacing the time commitment that I ordinarily would have devoted to classes and assignments.

The firm is a merit-based environment, so although I had the title of "Procurement Intern" I never felt that my position was "below" that of those around me. I directly supported seven employees based in The city and helped with ad-hoc analysis for another six members based out of the US. I feel that the firm co-ops serve as a form of onsite analysts or associates. It is uncommon for there to be entry-level positions for the firm within the US, and I think that co-ops have essentially replaced those roles within the city offices (2) and the New York office (1). The co-op program has been longstanding at the firm, with employing over a dozen college students since 2010. During my tenure at the firm, the number of co-ops employed averaged around 30 students.

Regarding company culture, I constantly felt like I was being spoiled by the opportunity to work for the firm, not only for their commitment to their clients but also to their employees. I have worked with a few different companies that were "client-oriented," but one of the main distinctions that I found with the firm was its dedication to following the advice it gives its clients. Considering it is a top management consulting firm, the firm operated with a complex matrix structure that relies on the employees' dedication to integrity, respect, collaboration, and constant improvement. Although a lot of companies pride themselves in work-life balance, I found that the firm was centered more on work-life separation. When you came into the office, you were on office time—where it was rare to even see someone on their phones or personal email. However, once people went home at the end of the day, it was expected for them to log off—and to focus on their personal time. People were often chastised by staying later or working on weekends, and it was anti-cultural to do so.

The firm has approximately 15,000 employees, with a complex matrix structure that is divided into geographic locations and departmental structure. They have 85 offices in 48 countries, with no exact "headquarters" location. However, the city 'Consulting Office' and the city 'Global Services' tend to be the closest equivalents (separate physical offices in downtown). Regarding commitment to co-ops or interns, I often felt that we were treated as if we were any other employees. One time I was working with a potential vendor, and I expressed to my team that the representative was a bit dismissive regarding communication because I was an intern. All of my team members instantly became defensive for me, requesting that I identify the vendor (I didn't), and they threatened to send stern emails to "stand up" for me.

Everyone was always supportive of my learning, people often taking time out of the day to teach me new things like SQL coding, or to spend time brainstorming solutions. Although my title was "Intern," I always felt like I had a "seat at the table" and I was constantly expected to offer input or to participate.

With complex matrix structures, decentralization is greatly applauded, but there are a few departments that cannot be efficient in a decentralized setup—one of them being procurement. With this in mind, I directly supported the North American Procurement team and indirectly supported the Global Procurement team (at the time a total of seventeen members). The procurement team falls under the Operations Services team that focuses on the global operations of the firm. Our primary focus was to negotiate savings with our vendors, ensuring that we are using vendors that best fulfill the company's needs for the lowest possible price. Considering the majority of the company spend came through Global Services, the procurement team is primarily based in that office.

I would say that the greatest struggle that my team struggled with was the decentralized nature of the company. To negotiate savings with all of our vendors, we need to be able to affect the spending throughout the company, which is difficult to do when everyone is accustomed to acting independently to fulfill their operating needs. As the analyst for the procurement team, I was responsible for creating and maintaining interactive dashboards that my team could use to negotiate savings with our larger vendors. Another obstacle that the company faced as a whole was being able to adjust and prepare enough for the fluctuations that occur within the marketplace. Whether it was new technological products or cybersecurity, the technological speed of the market was a constant pain point. Considering the amount of client information, we are responsible for, our security and discretion is paramount.

During my tenure at the firm, my day-to-day responsibilities would vary constantly. I would often devote time to fine-tuning the various dashboards that were constructed by myself and the prior co-op, which would include the total vendor spend throughout the entire company (discussed in further detail in the following question). I would also perform ad-hoc responsibilities like market research, running reports, and I created a tool that helped track the progress of the procurement team and their efforts.

As previously mentioned, one of my main responsibilities (the spend dashboards) was not created until after I accepted the position. When I initially interviewed, the job description had more basic requirements such as running reports or market research. However, upon onboarding, I realized that the job had changed completely upon the creation of these spend dashboards. Throughout the company, I was the only person who knew the structure behind these dashboards and the data analytic process that happened cyclically to produce this information. I would also run reports to validate the data and to continue developing it to ensure it could be used throughout the procurement team and the Operation Services team. Considering the development of these interactive and holistic spend dashboards was very recent, it was also my job to promote the use of these throughout the necessary parties in Finance, Operations, and IT. Other than maintaining this dashboard, I also created a reporting system for the procurement team that properly tracked the team's projects and the amount of money saved through their efforts.

Regarding collaboration with my team, I often relied on their input and feedback to adjust the spend dashboards and reporting tools so they can properly use them. Considering the procurement team was relatively new within the firm, I also worked with the team to find solutions for promoting awareness and expressing the importance of saving money for the company but also ensuring that my team is able to operate with the best efficiency.

Specific technical functions that my position called for were: a general understanding of SQL syntax and language structure, Excel fluency (please note this is very different from proficiency). I also learned basic HTML scripting throughout my internship to develop the savings reporting tool that I built for my team. Throughout my tenure, I also was working with "Big Data" and consistently worked with large databases that contained the entirety of the spend information throughout the company.

I would say that the only applicable academic concepts that came into play with my internship were my general understanding of how finances are reported throughout a company. However, the majority of the content that I worked on was not something I learned in any of my classes and created an incredibly steep learning curve.

Considering it was primarily an operations role, the main goals were all focused on ensuring the company was running smoothly or addressing any bottlenecks that were occurring. Procurement is primarily oriented toward saving the company money or maximizing savings, so most of the tasks that I was in charge of were ultimately save the company money.

Regarding data, I worked with Oracle databases daily and also used data analytics and visualization tools. I also worked with Excel constantly and needed to have an inherent understanding of how formulas and macros operate to be semi-fluent in using a few tools. I also created a tool within Sharepoint, so I developed an understanding of the coding behind SharePoint and how to manipulate it to produce the results I was looking for.

I didn't use too much machinery other than a basic Windows OS. Most of the skills that I had to develop were software development understanding.

Within my particular job description, I was expected to be a "data wizard." I was responsible for understanding the structure of our databases, their content, and how I could use this information to provide a user-friendly visualization tool. Considering I have never had any form of formal education regarding databases, I found that wrapping my head around the complexity of databases was one of the greatest struggles that I encountered. I often would discuss the structure and formation of these databases with members of IT and Finance to ensure that I had the proper understanding.

The firm operates primarily on providing information through slide decks. Throughout my tenure at the firm, I probably created an upward of 75 presentations that would eventually be shown to directors within the firm. These presentations varied from market research to RFQs. I also participated in creating protocol documents for vendor onboarding, focusing on risk and security measures taken before working with vendors.

Although I only received one form of written evaluation, I always expressed to my manager that I wanted as much feedback as possible, especially constructive feedback. Approximately once a month I would meet with my manager formally to assess my progress, but for the majority of my internship, I would always request immediate feedback or adjustments to my efforts. For the formal meetings, I would remind my manager a week in advance and would request that he get feedback from various team members that I work with -- requesting anonymity, so then they felt that they could give honest feedback. I found that by asking clarification questions and writing meticulous yet efficient notes, I was able to save time but also perform the necessary work. I also received a written assessment at the end of my co-op, which reflected the same findings from my feedback requests.

Working at the firm definitely helped me understand how important it is to have your personal values mirror those of the company that you work for. I pride myself on my constructive personal objectives, my work ethic to achieve these, and my philanthropy. Working at the firm helped me how crucial it is for me to work at a company that supports my personal values, but also helped me get exposure to

Operations and to see if I would like to pursue Operations in the future (I do).

Considering my classes are predetermined due to my specialty major, working at the firm didn't change my future coursework selection. However, one thing I did find was that it actually helped me holistically understand some of my classes, particularly my International Business and Organizational Behavior courses. Considering I experienced a lot of the ethical dilemmas that globalization brings (outsourcing, communication, solution strategies), I was able to understand how these can affect the day-to-day working environment. I also found that working for such an interesting and intrinsically rewarding company helped me understand that it is possible to find a company that fits your personal aspirations, and the sense of personal achievement affects you outside of the workplace.

Unfortunately, most of my classes were not helpful for this co-op. However, I would say that Financial Management and Managerial Accounting helped the most with understand the spend data that I used. Surprisingly enough, I found that Supply Chain (the closest academic course to Operations) was not helpful at all.

I find that the concepts that I have learned in school are not really applicable for people who want to work in "people-oriented" professions like myself. Most of my coursework involves learning about the stock market, company's financial statements, or measuring production output errors. However, knowing myself, none of these concepts are really helpful in the jobs that I am looking to pursue. I found that resolving social conflicts through mediation or compromise catered to my strengths but also addresses my personal values, and I have only found one course that addressed that.

I think that my co-op definitely matured and strengthened my technical expertise. I have found that my fluency in different operating systems has helped me improve my efficiency, but to also teach others how to improve their efforts to maximize time.

Even upon reflecting on my internship at the firm, I still feel personally satisfied with the work that I did. I had the opportunity to prove my abilities and capabilities to a great company and was able to grow and foster applicable skills for the future. I often recommend my position to others -- if I think that it aligns with their work ethic and skills. I am constantly thankful that I had the opportunity to work for the firm, and I have full intentions of pursuing a career with them in the future.

I think the main way that the co-op could be improved would be through a new job description considering all of the changes it underwent. However, I think that the amount of responsibility dedicated to the co-ops was crucial toward my personal satisfaction and should definitely be emphasized within the job description.

Interviewee #6 of 6

I worked for six months at an insurance company as a Continuous Improvement Analyst for the No-Fault and Central Billing Unit Departments within Claims. As a marketing major, this particular position was a means for me to explore opportunities outside of the boundaries of my major. Though there weren't many marketing-heavy tasks, the experience I gained translates into business skills I will need in the future. My education in marketing supplemented my projects, especially with goals set to improve customer experience.

The co-op program has been integrated thoroughly for quite some time with the company, but my specific co-op position was new. I was one of two co-ops hired by my manager for the Continuous

Improvement position during the fall. Given the amount of work allocated to the other co-op, and me, I think my manager needed a couple of extra hands on deck. The company held co-op events once a month where we listened to keynote speakers from the company, ranging from executives to community service leaders. They made an effort in creating a company co-op network, and through these events, I was able to meet other co-ops. I learned through hearing others' experiences that many were hired alone, without another co-op on the team. Before our arrival, the company had also hired a wave of summer interns. From my experience, I gathered that the company values college students and views them as potential hires. My manager, Ben Fisher, treated us as full-time employees, rather than co-ops, assigning us projects that had the potential to have a great impact on processes in Claims. Even though this was his first experience leading co-ops, he did an incredible job shaping us into becoming valuable employees.

The company is an extremely large organization with branches spreading all over the states. My mentor worked out of the local office, and our check-ins were done over Skype once a week. In fact, the majority of people I collaborated with were not located in the city, but I never saw this as an obstacle, especially with the capabilities of screen sharing on Skype. The company's structure was hierarchical; I was very aware of who reported to whom. This didn't come to my surprise for a corporate company, especially after my previous position at a financial services firm. As mentioned before, the company made an effort in creating an environment in which co-ops could network and foster professional relationships. This eased the burden of seeking out other co-ops on my own. The company held community service events, in which the co-ops helped pack medical supplies for charities. Additionally, we were invited to the company outing with other Claims employees to help expand our professional network. Finally, the company offered co-ops flexible time-off, which was something I did not have at my previous co-op. Company gestures like these helped me feel respected and valued, even as a co-op.

I reported to the Director of Claims Operations and my mentor, an LMS Analyst, also reported to my manager. We were a branch of the Claims Department, more specifically the Operations of Central Billing Unit and No-Fault divisions. As a co-op, we were able to see the gears of such a large organization as the company function.

Ultimately, the Operations team's goal was to make any and all processes related to Claims as efficient as possible, identifying pain points and generating solutions to address these challenges. These challenges ranged from Tier 1 to Tier 4; Tier 1 focusing on one specific branch location and Tier 4 applying to issues identified in a national, company-wide level. One of my largest projects was picking a CI (Continuous Improvement Idea), an idea that was proposed by a Claims Adjustor to help improve a process. My specific CI was an idea to improve the efficiency of updating requests into the Claims system. The issue stemmed from the lack of communication and information between an adjustor and a nurse manager. Requests were getting marked read by an adjuster on the Claims system without proper nurse manager approval. This led to a delay in payment and could potentially lead to procedures done in a hospital without the customer knowing whether the procedure would be covered by insurance. I worked on a cross-functional team, working with the adjustors, the nurse managers, members of the product team, as well as the IT team. My proposed solution was to bridge the gap between the adjustors and the nurse managers. I created an information sheet consisting of what and why the issue existed in an attempt to spread awareness of the problem. The biggest challenge I faced during this project was the slow progression of the process; many of whom I spoke with were busy with other tasks and finding a time to speak was difficult. Ultimately, this illuminated the challenges of developing an idea from conception to implementation.

This co-op consisted mainly of Excel visual reporting from various metrics to provide visibility into the pain points and overall health of the NF and CBU operations. Many responsibilities were ad-hoc; if there was a quarterly meeting coming up, we were charged with compiling our visual reports onto PowerPoint. There were many weekly or bi-weekly updates that we were expected to make compiled from data collected over the past week or the past two weeks. This took the majority of my time especially since the visual reports that were created needed multiple people's approvals and many times changes needed to be made. Other than these scheduled projects, our manager, kept us busy supporting larger scale projects he was working on. These projects were very Excel heavy and ranged from a one day deadline to two months.

Our job description mainly consisted of providing support for the Claims Operations unit. Going into the job, I did not know exactly what to expect. The largest project I took on beyond my job description was creating a system for incorporating customer feedback to improve our customer service. After a customer submits a Claim or has an exchange with an adjuster, they are asked what they thought of the service; a quick survey to gauge their experience. Previously, this feedback was not utilized or reviewed extensively. I began working on a project to utilize this feedback. Initially, I had to manually scrub the data, creating a second spreadsheet that consisted of positive comments and negative comments, specific adjustors that received praise or constructive criticisms, and reoccurring concerns that the customers expressed. Unfortunately, my time at the company ended before I was able to complete this project but another member of the team picked it up where I left off. When I left, I was able to create a macro that organized the data received from these surveys to pull keywords such as "rude" or "slow" or "helpful." By doing so, it helped eliminate the need to read through hundreds of surveys. I would have loved to continue this project as I felt a sense of pride for the work I was doing and the feedback I was receiving.

The other co-op and I worked together nearly every day for the first month or two. We were given one large assignment and would divvy up parts and collaborate with others. The largest project we worked on together was creating an automated master spreadsheet that the LMS Analysts had to update every month. We linked this spreadsheet to pivot tables that could be adjusted with new data as it was inputted. Previously, the visual reports had to be built manually every month, but we created a way to save time for the LMS Analysts to be able to push one button and have these graphs updated. Working with a colleague was very helpful. Thankfully, he was very easy to work with and the strengths he had complimented my strengths. As an industrial engineer, his analytical thinking differed from mine, and when working together, we heightened each other's strengths.

As time went on, my work became more independent, and I began to diverge with my projects. There were larger scale projects, such as a monthly report out that we worked on together, but other than those, we were assigned different tasks. With that said, I always had the support of my fellow co-op and could use him as a resource and vice versa.

My position required very heavy Excel knowledge. Before my entry, I had limited skills in Excel, but my manager was very understanding and encouraged us to learn through trial and error. We guided us when our experience fell short, and Google was our greatest resource. By the second or third month, I felt very comfortable with Excel. Additionally, there were some functions h knew that I didn't and vice versa; it was incredibly helpful to have two brains these technical problems.

I never felt that there was any explicit academic knowledge needed to succeed in my position. The team I worked with was very supportive. Learning new software such as Excel took time and patience and I think taking the initiative, being patient, and having a good work ethic yielded a successful co-op.

I began every project with a drive to produce the best work I could. I know that as co-ops, we might have been held to a lower standard, but I wanted to prove that I could be just as valuable as a co-op than any other employee. I made sure to always ask for feedback and ensured I incorporated it into the following assignments. I learned that my manager and my mentor and other people I worked with were always willing to help or show me a new way of doing things and I appreciated their words as I know it made me a better colleague and would help me yield the most from my co-op experience.

Much of our data was internally generated, and we used Microsoft Excel to analyze and build visual reports from this data. Once these visual reports were built, Microsoft PowerPoint was the most common means to present our work.

While building the visual reports, I relied heavily on pivot tables, V-lookups, macros, and many more functions provided by Excel.

My two largest projects were my CI regarding updating requests into the Claims system and a system to support incorporating customer feedback. My CI was not very data heavy but my second project relied heavily on analysis of data. As mentioned before, I built a macro to help analyze the data to pull keywords in an attempt to make the data analysis more timely and efficient.

I had two opportunities to meet my manager's manager. She was the Manager of Operations for CBU, NF, and SIU units. We were given an opportunity to build a PowerPoint to update her on our work and projects and receive feedback. These were the highest-pressure presentations I had, and I prepared for weeks to give a 30-minute presentation. Her feedback was incredibly valuable, and this experience gave me insight into what to expect during a professional presentation. She eased the tension and was extremely easy to speak to. Other than these two presentations, I was expected to create a document for the implementation of my CI.

I had a weekly meeting with my manager and another weekly check-in with my mentor for updating them on the progress of my projects and receiving feedback. During these meetings, I was given feedback on my work. The evaluation I received was very positive, and they were happy to be put down as a reference for future career steps I would take. My manager and I read through my written evaluation, and I was extremely pleased with the kind words he had to say. He did have one point of constructive criticism, and that was to be more assertive with my work. Going into the position I was very shy and working with someone who is very outgoing, my manager mentioned that there were a couple times my fellow co-op had a stronger presence than me in the room. Moving forward, this will be my main point of improvement.

My experience at the company shifted my career goals and helped narrow my focus. I never knew exactly what job I wanted, but through the co-op program at my university, I have a better idea of what I do not want. I find that just as valuable. Moving forward, I am hoping to gain more experience in the industry that I have been interested in. Frankly, while I was going through my co-op interviews, I sacrificed my interests in the entertainment industry for the security of a higher-paying position at a corporate company.

Though I learned much about myself and gained exposure to a professional working environment, my biggest regret is allowing safety and security to overshadow my passion. With this knowledge, I realized that I should pursue my interests and my passions, especially at my age since I am still learning and growing. I want to gain as much experience and exposure to help shape my future career goals. I am happy to say that my curiosity in working for a large corporate company has been satisfied and I can move forward knowing I am not missing on opportunities.

After my two co-ops, I realized that the knowledge gained from textbooks and the knowledge gained at my co-op is vastly different. With that said, moving forward, my future coursework will be centered on specific aspects of marketing, such as digital marketing and advertising and communications. Though my time at the company did not touch on these topics, it made me want to explore these much more. I am an avid learner and still very young with much to learn. I am excited about the continued experience both academically and professionally.

I wish I had taken Organizational Behavior before my second co-op experience. Concepts we learned in this class will resonate with me throughout my professional career, and I am thankful to have this knowledge.

The education I received at my university was theoretical but that coupled with my other work experiences allowed me to learn the ropes. In school, we are very much guided through our assignments, told exactly what is expected and how to get an "A." During my co-op, I was given an assignment and was expected to produce the results my manager was looking for. Granted, we were given some guidance when we asked.

To be frank, all the technical skills I learned from this co-op I learned on the job. I think that in and of itself was a great learning experience since I realized that even without any technical experience or education, it was possible for me to pick up the skills needed to succeed at my co-op.

My colleague, an industrial engineering major, found this co-op to be very rewarding and was able to exercise the concepts he learned in class throughout the co-op. I, on the other hand, as a marketing major, found the position fell short of what I wanted. I did gain invaluable knowledge and experience, and this will make me a better employee in the future, which is why I don't regret taking this position. I just wish I was able to gain heavier mentorship in marketing aspects.

Overall, I think the co-op was great, especially for my manager's first time hiring a co-op. This was not a position for marketing students searching for marketing experience, but in hindsight, I am glad I took this position for the Excel experience I gained.

CHAPTER 7

ENTREPRENEURSHIP

ABOUT ENTREPRENEURS AND WORKING WITH THEM

To many, becoming an entrepreneur might seem like a scary and high-risk journey, but to some of us, this unpredictable adventure looks like the perfect path our life should take. Entering the challenging world of entrepreneurship is probably the only way for some people who hate their jobs to change their circumstances and be successful. Successful people inspire other people to become successful. Many hopefuls believe that becoming an entrepreneur will allow us to network with—and become like—people who have already built great businesses. We think that we have enough potential to find the next profitable idea and change the lives of millions, or more importantly... our own. Seeing someone with nothing, grow to become a successful businessperson is often the motivation for aspiring entrepreneurs to start their own businesses.

How Do You Spot an Entrepreneur in Hiding?

Some people struggle with respecting authority. They don't like the reality of having people in superior positions managing their work and looking over their shoulder. Not having the final say in important decisions turns them off, so they seek opportunities where they can have more control over business operations. Even though they don't like authority figures, they believe that becoming their own boss is the only way that they can do work effectively and happily. The reality of working an average job doesn't seem rewarding to aspiring entrepreneurs. Having to finish unfulfilling tasks seems really boring to them. Getting coffee and greeting nice co-workers every morning gets boring after a while. The repetitive and routine nature of working 9 to 5 doesn't feed their burning passion for creativity and innovation. They feel like they are merely doing what society expects of them instead of making a difference in the world. It's through starting their own business that they get to freely express their creative ideas and fulfill their dreams.

Building a successful business takes risk, and we entrepreneurs love risks! We live for excitement and adventure. Brainstorming new ideas and gambling their chance of succeeding in their target market gives them goosebumps. We look to manage projects with high stakes because they have enough confidence to execute them. Whether these projects become million-dollar success stories or complete failures that they regret, it's the act of betting on an idea and watching it develop that makes aspiring entrepreneurs smile.

Some people become entrepreneurs because they see it as a journey they must make. Their prior experience in the job market or achievements in education makes them realize that working for others is no longer a life suited for them. A fire in our hearts tells us that we have a definite purpose in the world that surpasses the reality of being an employee. Entrepreneurs are driven by the need to succeed and control their own destiny. Owning a business gives us no limitations on the profit and opportunities that we can gain.

Are You Sure You Want to Be an Entrepreneur?

Simply put, entrepreneurs are people who choose to run their own company rather than work as employees. An entrepreneur is someone who creates a business from scratch, through literal blood, sweat, and tears with all the risks and rewards it implies. What an entrepreneur fundamentally does is identify a need and fill it.

Entrepreneurs dream and make their dreams come true. It is my personal conviction that entrepreneurship cannot be learned or taught. You will never see a successful entrepreneur who is negative or does not believe in what they do. Entrepreneurship is either an inner quality or something that's entirely foreign to you. It is not a job or a hobby; it's a lifestyle and a state of mind.

Because entrepreneurs face challenges and never give up, they have to adapt and take action. Every action you take, as an entrepreneur should serve a purpose that will help you grow your business, and become better at what you do.

CO-OP PARTICIPANT INTERVIEWS

Interviewee #1 of 4

I worked at an optometry startup company that provided mobile eye care to various companies in the city area. I worked there for six months full-time then was re-hired after my co-op to work part-time (one to two days per week). This allowed me to really see the arc of startup growth. When I began my co-op, the company was located in a garage, and by the time I left a few weeks ago, we were located in the city with a much more formalized office. When I was hired, my position was called Client Coordinator Co-Op. My job description stated I would be assisting client coordinators to manage client interactions and ensure that the mobile eye events went smoothly. My role would rapidly evolve and shift from this description, but I accepted the job with the understanding that I would be working as a liaison with clients as well as helping with general operations tasks. This fit with my business degree, which at the time was Business Administration with a management concentration, as well as a degree in political science. I hoped to utilize my people skills while at the same time gaining some needed hard business skills.

I was included in the first round of co-ops the organization had ever hired. They hired five co-ops. Two client coordination, one sales, one marketing, and one design co-op. For four out of the five co-ops, it was our first co-op at my university. My client coordinator position itself was a very valuable asset to the company because the client coordinators are the most public face of the company. They network with clients and deal with any sort of customer service issues. The company was still very young, and co-ops provided a mode of cheap, hirable labor. The co-op program provided relatively reputable talent, and since we could be paid hourly without formal benefits, it was a good fiscal decision for the organization.

The company also prided itself on transparency and equality, however, as my co-op continued these values started to be called into question. The culture definitely carried the "work hard, play hard" mentality with many employees getting in before eight and staying past six. However, company happy hours or cracking beers at five were very normal among colleagues. The overall demographic was young 20s-30s with many of the employees working their first full-time post-college job.

The company was approximately forty employees with about twenty-five in headquarters. The organizational structure changed throughout my time with the company, but the basic structure consisted of six main branches sales, operations (client coordination), marketing, finance, expansion, and the medical team. Each of these branches had an executive board member that was in charge of the branch, and then the CEO presided over the executive board. The sales team was by far the largest department with about 6-8 business development agents when I was hired. Client coordination was composed of two members before co-ops, the marketing team and the finance team had only one member each (not including the executive board members). Expansion was only composed of one executive member. The medical team was the largest team and was made of optometrists, store managers, and ophthalmic technicians that worked on a rotating basis based on the scheduled appointments. Since the company was so small and the co-op program was so new to the company, co-ops were quite valued and were not treated differently from other employees.

My position was housed strictly in the operations portion of the company. As a client coordination co-op, I quickly became an assistant of sorts to the existing client coordinators. I was tasked to learn as much as I could about the position so that I could start to relieve some of their workloads and eventually have my own clients. I worked extremely closely with the other client coordination co-op as well as with the finance director because a lot of the client coordination responsibilities had to do with insurance and insurance reimbursements. The longer I stayed with the company, however, the more exposure I got to other departments. The culture in the company was very fluid, so if I had free time, I could take on projects in other areas of the business.

Since profitability is based on employees of companies signing up for eye exams the main goal throughout my time at the organization was to boost customer engagement. This fell heavily on the client coordination team who had to work closely with HR professionals to design strategies to get their employees to sign up for eye exams. This proved extremely difficult. Some company cultures loved getting frequent emails, other companies would not allow for regular emails, and so the client coordination team had to get creative. One of my main responsibilities was running a meeting addressing the progress we had made on any creative tactics and assigning various co-workers to companies that were not performing well so that they could focus on driving engagement for that particular company.

My day-to-day activities are quite difficult to describe because I was at the mercy of the client coordination team and the clients they were dealing with at the time. When I first began my primary duty was performing insurance eligibility checks to ensure that our patients were able to receive eye exams with the organization. This could take up to a full day, but often I did eligibility checks in the morning and special projects in the afternoon. Special projects included email campaigns, evaluating the pricing structure of glasses, obtaining parking permits, and performing customer service tasks.

One of the main duties I took on that was beyond my standard job description was that of inventory. Two or three months into my co-op an operations assistant quit leaving the company with no one to manage the inventory of glasses frames. Since I was growing tired of eligibility checks and repeated paperwork completing inventory was a welcome change, and I continued to monitor the inventory until I left about a year later. Additionally, I embarked on a special trip to Atlanta to operate optician equipment when during expansion the company did not have an employee to serve their first clients in the area.

Nearly every activity I completed was done in a project team or with co-workers. The nature of the company was to always pair up and have multiple hands working on one project. If I was doing a project by myself, I always had opportunities to check-in with my supervisor or reach out for assistance if I needed it. At the same time, I had a lot of independence. For example, when dealing with customer service inquiries, I was empowered to do whatever needed to be done to ensure the customer left happy even if that meant offering a significant discount. My biggest project was creating an explanation of benefits where we took company insurance plans and modified them so that the customer understood what buying glasses or contacts would cost them through the organization. The explanation of benefits was constantly being modified, and I worked on them repeatedly with the marketing, finance, and operations team throughout my time at the organization.

My position was not largely technical although I did need to become familiar with the company's Electronic Medical Records (EMR) system to complete eligibility checks and maintain the inventory.

My computer fundamentals course was my most helpful course because I had to complete a lot of work with spreadsheets and had to be comfortable with a PC. My political science classes had helped with my writing skills which came in handy when dealing with clients and customers. Many of my basic business courses such as accounting and finance did not apply to this particular position, but I was able to better understand the company's standings because of my experience in those classes.

The projects I was involved in centered on profitability and customer retention as their primary goals. One project involved me determining the proper pricing structure for glasses when we served clients without network insurance. Another project was designing a cost-effective reminder call system to reduce the number of patient no-show rates. Client coordination was all about making the customers happy and get them to encourage their HR teams to bring the organization back on site.

For the glasses cost project, I designed a spreadsheet that calculated pricing and profits to ensure that if we cut costs to match an insurance plan we were not losing too much money. It was a simple operation that allowed our team to visualize profits and losses. The other primary software was the EMR record system used for eye exams and inventory. I also had to make use of Salesforce.com to track the client events.

Data was not an important part of my work at the organization. Often, I had to build my own data to support my projects because I was working on projects that had not been worked on before. In the case of the reminder call project, I had to record all of my calls to support the need for an automated calling solution.

Most of my work was creating materials on behalf of client coordination. I filled in email campaigns and set up web pages for sign-ups. I made a couple presentations to the executive team, but those were of my own volition and not required of me to complete. Since I was in operations, most of my work did not require formalized documents or presentations and instead was about maintenance of regular activities.

The co-op program builds in an evaluation to the end of the co-op process. That was the primary form of assessment I received for my work throughout my co-op. The assessment discussed my special projects, my ability to work with others, and an evaluation of if I met the goals I set for myself at the beginning of my co-op. I also had one-on-one meetings with my supervisor on a weekly or bi-weekly basis. These meetings served as check-ins for her to understand what I had been working on, what I wanted to work on, and what I was having trouble with. I was thankful for the written assessment at the end because it concretely stated things we had talked about in our one-on-one meetings. Other members of the team did not formally assess my work and instead reported any compliments or complaints to my boss.

This job has been a huge opportunity for me to find out what I want to do when I graduate. I learned that I love working with people and managing projects. I learned how to speak with executive leadership and how to stay on top of multiple projects at once. My biggest learning experience, however, was learning about startup life. I had always assumed that I would thrive in the startup environment.

While I loved some aspects of the culture, the never-ending workflow took a toll on my co-workers and me. My next co-op is a very established company, and I am excited to see how I like being in a co-op position where many co-ops have come before me, and there are clear expectations. I've learned that I can rise to the occasion in startups, but now the co-op program is giving me a chance to see if it is the best fit for my career. Without the co-op program, I would not have learned about my personal work ethic in a job setting until after graduation.

During my time at the organization, I realized that operations was not the place I wanted to be in long-term with a company. I was very drawn to sales and marketing during my time with the company, and this inspired me to change my concentration from management to marketing. I feel like I can learn a lot about management from observing leaders in my further co-op experiences while marketing classes will expose me to the specific strategies I need to thrive post-graduation. I have already taken marketing specific classes, and I enjoy them very much.

The most applicable course to my first co-op was my computer fundamentals course because it allowed me to use my PC with ease and adapt quickly to the clunky EMR and the ins and outs of Salesforce. Some of my least applicable courses were my political science courses such as American Government. However, I do believe that the essays I had to write for those classes strengthened my overall competency. When I started my first co-op, I had not actually taken many courses within the School of Business because I did not declare my business major until the end of my first year.

Nothing in the classroom prepares you for the personal interactions you will face on the job. I had to learn how each and every one of my co-workers acted so that I could communicate with them properly and earn their respect. Co-op also puts into perspective what is important in the classroom. It's not about every grade or every moment in class, and instead, it's about building a toolkit that can be used no matter what job you go into and who you can work with. After co-op, I have valued my class time so much more, but I have also taken a class with a softer perspective surrounded by less pressure because a career is built slowly and not just in the classroom.

I put my technical background to use, but I do not think that my co-op forced me to use my technical background. Often, I was bringing as much as I could to the table so that I could gain more responsibility within the organization. If I did not push myself, I think I would have been continually doing very mundane tasks.

I learned so much during my co-op. I loved so many aspects. At times it was difficult and tedious but that is part of life and by stretching myself and speaking up when I was not content I got so much out of my work with the organization. I gained so much more confidence in my public speaking abilities as well as my networking skills. I got more comfortable with PCs instead of Macs, and I built relationships that will help me in my career going forward. I would recommend my co-op to others, and I would definitely recommend that anyone considering working at a startup should try a co-op to see if that lifestyle fits their true wants and needs.

The company needs a much more formalized co-op structure because what I did during my co-op was completely different from the job description I signed up for. I never ended up directly working with a client or having my own clients even though I would have been able to handle the workload and present the company in a good light. My boss was also remote for a lot of the time I worked at the organization, and that is very hard for a co-op to have a fluid structure and no formal leadership in place. I had to do a lot of my own projects and seek out work from other departments. Co-op is what you make of it, but I found that most of my learning was not in the projects or technical skills themselves but were about company culture and company values. How to work and thrive in an organization largely comes down to how you can work with and lead people. They should probably not be a company that continues with the co-op program if they cannot make it so that co-ops have formalized roles and responsibilities because otherwise co-ops are left overworked or dissatisfied.

Interviewee #2 of 4

For the entrepreneurship, I worked in two different companies -- completing two internships in different departments. For the sake of organization, I will be indicating which company I am referring to with an "AN" for one co-op and "CB" for the second, or "Both" if my statement is this co-op networks for my first internship as their HR Intern. I worked with them for 3 months immediately out of high school. CB: I worked at CB for my fourth internship as a Business Development Intern for 3 months during my second semester junior year in the city. Considering I was still taking classes during this, I worked about 20 hours a week.

AN: Considering I was the youngest and least experienced employee by a large margin, my job was essentially ornery, the work that I was performed hardly affected the company in any significant way and primarily consisted of administrative work. However, they did have a very developed internship program, and I was able to participate in arranging the events and coordinating with the marketing team to further promote the internship program.

CB: Similarly, to the AN role, I didn't find much significance in the work that I was doing at CB. I was primarily doing cold calls, so the impact of my efforts was negligible. The co-op program at CB has been going for a few years, primarily in the engineering teams, but I was part of a new initiative of bringing on co-ops in the Sales and HR teams.

AN: They very much embraced the Silicon Valley startup mentality, with a very casual environment where people would have their dogs or children come to the office, and it was considered socially unacceptable to be at work after 2 pm on a Friday. The greatest takeaway that I got from the company's values was actually their client-prioritization. The CEO iterated the idea that all efforts should be made with the 'Customer first, customer last.' All work should be started and ended with the customer in mind, ensuring that all efforts tie back to the customer.

CB: The company environment was actually very similar to Aruba Networks'. They had a strong focus on creating a relaxing work environment and prided themselves on the perks that they offered.

AN: Unfortunately, I don't know how many employees the company had at this point, and they were acquired by another company, so I don't have many resources to deduct the company size during the time that I worked there. However, I found that they were very committed to the interns, and we often would have lunch with various C-Suite executives, and there were a lot of networking opportunities at all company events.

CB: There were approximately 800 employees by the time that I joined. However they still behaved very much like a startup, and the CEO would often walk up to any employees and just would have conversations with employees -- myself included.

AN: I supported the manager of the Immigration and Relocation sector of HR.

CB: I was considered the equal standing as a Business Development Representative -- who ultimately rolled up to the Inside Sales

Manager who would report to the VP of Sales. Both: The company was broken up by departments and had a linear reporting system.

AN: One of the greatest challenges that the company faced was the presence of larger competitors. At the time, the greatest challenge was establishing enough clout to compete with the larger enterprise clients that were either with the competitor or reconsidering them. Another obstacle that they faced was the fact that they were constantly looking hiring and would have to go through tedious and mundane efforts to comply with legal requirements.

CB: One of the greatest difficulties as a whole is the presence of similar products like Google Drive, which essentially are more user-friendly, and immediately rewarding compared to the cloud backup solution we offered.

AN: My duties were not the most exciting -- often devoting the whole day to resume evaluation for open positions, interview arranging, and event preparation for internship-related events.

CB: I was responsible for cold calling various lists -- ones that we either purchased or older prospects that we lost touch with. By the second month, I was averaging around 80-90 calls per day.

AN: I originally was only meant to be going through the various resumes throughout the workday, but once that became too easy to do, I collaborated with fellow interns to create a marketing intern to promote the internship program.

CB: Very similarly to AN, once I found that I was able to fulfill my calling quota, I started looking around to help out with additional work. I ended up supporting the Sales Operations team for a brief period of time, in assuring customer satisfaction and working to pull reports for the sales team.

AN: The most collaborative project that I worked on at AN was the marketing video that I was working on. Other than that, I primarily was expected to go through about 60 resumes a day and sort them according to whether or not they were considered candidates. CB: None of my work was collaborative.

AN: The only technical requirements were a general understanding of Word and Excel, and then closer to the end of my internship I started working with Workday (but not enough to be proficient). CB: The technical side of my position consisted of navigating Salesforce, and using my fluency in the Windows OS to help create usable reports for the sales members when necessary.

Both: Considering they were very socially oriented positions, I didn't find that anything I learned in school was actually applicable toward my success in these positions. All of the required skills had to be learned throughout my internships -- whether it was basic Excel skills or certain sales strategies.

AN: The goal of my work was to ensure that the best possible candidates were being hired.

CB: My primary objective was to gauge interest from my cold calls, and if any of them seemed interested in our product, I would suggest that they start a free trial and then I would escalate them to a Channel Sales Manager.

Both: Neither of these positions required special software other than Workday and Adobe Reader and Salesforce.

AN: I only needed to know how to use Microsoft Office products.

CB: I used Microsoft Office products as well as the calling platform that we used to for our call system. I actually found the calling platform to be one of the least flexible systems that I have ever worked with, causing calls to be constantly dropped and an average of 2 hours of call time was lost due to the calling platform issues across the sales department. However, I think the reason why we continued to use the calling platform was that a better product would have been too expensive.

AN: No data other than the job descriptions and the requirements that we were looking for in candidates.

CB: I didn't work with as much data in this particular role. Considering I was in sales, I did need to be fluent in the product offering and the differences among the different products offered.

Both: Considering these internships were shorter, I was not required to complete any documents or interviews other than basic off-boarding measures.

AN: During my time, I found that although my work wasn't very skill-based, one of the things that I was commended for was my ability to work efficiently. My manager often praised my ability to socialize with many people and that I was able to create work when there was a deficit of work assignments.

CB: At the end of my time, I didn't receive a written evaluation, but I did have multiple conversations with my manager, and he really stressed how impressed he was with my work ethic and professionalism.

AN: Considering this was my first internship, I was able to experience the corporate setting and get a proper understanding of what a career could look like in that setting. I also realized that although I was able to be content with my administrative work, I preferred when my work was more outward facing. For following jobs, I have been able to take my personal understanding of my needs and have looked for more outward facing roles since then.

CB: One of the main reasons that I chose to work for CB was because I wanted to have experience in sales. It had always seemed like a potential career path for me, but I knew I would need to have to actually do it to determine whether or not I would like it. Although I knew I was joining a company that maybe didn't align with my personal values perfectly, I decided that the practical occupation experience was worth some discomfort.

AN: Upon working in HR, I found that I was definitely meant to work in some corporate-type occupation. Although I was self-reflective enough to decide that I would succeed in Business, working in the corporate environment encouraged and reaffirmed my decision.

CB: By the time I worked at the company, I didn't really have any flexibility in my future coursework, but it did reaffirm my thoughts that I would not have been able to determine whether or not I would like sales until I actually got practical experience in it.

AN: I think that with this internship, the most applicable course that I took for this was my entry class into the corporate workplace (the co-op preparation class). Although my internship happened two years before actually taking the class, I would have found the information provided to have been very helpful if I had taken it sooner.

CB: I feel like one of the greatest shortcomings with Business Schools is that they don't teach one of the largest departments that fall within businesses (sales). Although I think that it is something you need to learn from the first-hand experience, I wish there was a better way of including it within my course curriculum. I think one of the greatest distinctions between the course I have taken and these internships is that none of my classes have had relevant teachings toward these departments. Although there are HR classes offered at my university, they are not requirements, and I think that many students could benefit from learning about some of the challenges that are faced, particularly with Diversity, Recruiting, and Immigration. In regards to sales, there is literally no class that has covered any of the things that I learned during my internship, and I think that is actually a really flawed shortcoming that is common among most business classes.

AN: Considering my inexperience with technology at the time, I think that this role was great for my entry into the working environment.

CB: I actually found that my technical skills that I had developed before this position went to waste. The work that I was doing required very few technical skills, and I found that I often was called over to teach my co-workers how to simplify or optimize their use of the applicable software.

AN: At the time I felt incredibly satisfied by the job (which I think might have been because I didn't have anything to compare it to). I actually went on to accept another position in HR as a Recruiting Intern at another after this internship. Although I decided to stray from Human Resources, I still think that my social understanding of the time and efforts of members of HR was important to understand the social issues that companies face. However, I wouldn't suggest that this becomes a co-op position because there was not a sufficient number of substantial tasks throughout the day for there to be conducive learning.

CB: I actually really struggled with this job personally. Working part-time had its own challenges with a full-time course load, but I found that the concept of cold calling people went against my own personal values. I think that someone else who is able to reframe his or her personal needs and values within employment would succeed in this position. I think that the company has a very clear mission in mind, it just happened to be asymmetric with my own personal values, and

I wasn't able to overlook the discontentment I found in my day-to-day tasks.

CB: I think that something that could be improved would be more of a rotary focus on the different types of sales within the company. Although cold calling gives you the most immediate experience, I think that experimenting with the different sales types is important to get a good understanding of the different roles throughout the department.

Interviewee #3 of 4

I secured a co-op position inside the company where I completed my first co-op. I was a sophomore, and it was mid-November. All of my friends had secured a position at some firm or another weeks ago, and I was having mild heart attacks as each day passed where I still remained jobless. To further my rising anxiety, I had only applied to three jobs, because the pool of internships on the university co-op job board just didn't entice me. Two of those applications were for the company. The first was a singular opening in their school on the West Coast which was new and competitive, and the second in their headquarters among 39 other interns reviewing applications for six months which was the furthest from my cup of tea as one could get.

The third was for a Social Enterprise Incubator that had fallen through days before due to strife with the current interns. Basically, I had put all of my eggs in one basket, which all depended on the Skype interview I got with the school director later that week. I had always wanted to do a Skype interview like in the movies, and while now was definitely not the time to try it, 19-year old me did not consider that. I sat there in my underwear and a dress shirt, enthusiastically describing my passion for travel and education to the man on the other side of my phone screen - my computer suffered from chronic and such perfectly timed technological issues. I nervously watched the battery life descend from 50 to 40 to 10 percent. Thank GOD the interview wrapped up as it hit 1% because I was not in the right attire to stand up and grab my phone charger.

Many lessons were learned that day, including the one that sometimes, if you show just how much you want the position through the passion in your words and your face, they might just email you back 3 hours later with the job offer and contract attached. So within two months, I was leaving the West Coast with a suitcase and my guitar (so classic California it almost hurts) and moving into a city where I knew basically no one for the next six months.

The company is a world leader in international education, whose mission aims to open the world through education. They have offices and schools around the world, providing a variety of services to thousands of students a year. While it's an enormous global company of over 40,000 employees, the West Coast office felt far removed from the strict corporate expectations. The office is an international that teaches English to 500 students at any given time, ranging from 18-80 years old, from over 50 countries around the world. Students come from across the globe to the school to learn the language and get an authentic American experience. Thirteen admin staff run the school, working in four departments: Academics, Student Services, Activities, and Housing. Respectively, the departments dealt with class schedules and grading; visas and legal logistics; fun activities to do in and around the city; and housing in a dorm or host family.

Housing was my home base department, although there was always so much to do that everyone had a hand in everywhere. My role was the Host Family Recruitment co-op, working under the Host Family Coordinator in our team of four. My other two colleagues were Housing Coordinator (for dorm style living situations) and Housing Director, a woman who had been with the company longer than anyone in the school, which was impressive because of the high turnover rate. But didn't say too much as the oldest admin was 32, and most people had only been there for about a year.

My role was to find a few dozen new host families in and around the city to host the ever-expanding student population. Everybody informed me that I was doomed from the start. My mission was to convince locals - the most expensive cities to rent in the country - to provide a warm and loving environment to a foreign student (or 2 or 6) for 2-52 weeks for a $300 food stipend per week. "Good Luck," they told me. So, I got to work. I rang every old or new-and-forgotten phone number in the database that we had acquired, emailed every address, and tried to forge new partnerships with every local organization, school, and religious/cultural center in the city. It was a challenging task, and while I did gain a surprising number of responses and conduct a good amount of home inspection visits, ultimately, the number of interested hosts to the goal number of hosts EF wanted didn't match up. I was disappointed that I didn't attain the 70+ host family mark, but I also recognized that this unrealistic number and pressure to perform the impossible from upper management was the reason the previous Host Family Coordinator had abruptly left the company.

The New England HQ of the company hires about 40 co-ops each cycle, in a variety of internal departments. I was the first co-op that the West Coast office had ever had, and so for the first couple of months, the director didn't know how responsible I was and didn't assign me a large workload until I demonstrated my capabilities. My role had advertised recruiting host families, organizing events and assisting other departments with whatever other work is necessary. My first big 'test' as an intern was organizing the belated company holiday party for 100 people (the staff, teachers, and +1s) 2 weeks before it was expected to take place. I love to organize events, and I work best under pressure, so it was an enjoyable project. It ended up being so successful that they hosted the next year's holiday party there again.

From there I began to gain more responsibilities. A portion of my role involved maintaining current student bookings, assisting current students with any issues they may have, and facilitating weekly intake of new students. Another portion involved assisting the activities department, where I'd create monthly event calendars for students to explore the city and lead certain events, like a baseball game or skydiving. I'd organize events and assist with the facilitation of company events as needed. However, my core role was based on recruitment. I would recruit new host families through a variety of platforms and channels (i.e., email, craigslist, Facebook and Meet-up, etc.), screen those individuals who were interested, conduct home visits, accept or reject their applications, and allocate new students to them. The previous employee in the role, who had been there for years and understood all partnerships, host family relationships, and specific business processes within the school, had taken all of that knowledge with her when she left. As a result, it was as if my colleague, the Host Family Coordinator, who had only begun shortly before I had, and myself were starting from scratch. I made efforts to establish a basis of processes for what I did and create a recruitment handbook for the position in future years. I updated the current processes to allow for more effective host family-student communication. I had taken a Foundations of Computer Science course my previous semester, and it was a gratifying feeling improving the weekly and daily processes with a (now) simple vlookup formula. By the close of my six months, I was creating work calendars for the summer Outreach Coordinator team that I had recruited, screened, and assisted in hiring and training, and while my performance in specifically recruitment did not meet goal (expectedly), the school director informed me that I the best intern he'd ever had.

This self-establishment of my role most likely contributed to why my experience felt more working for a startup than the vast corporation it is. Combined with the buzz of students walking around the halls, the hands-on events we'd organize and facilitate ourselves, and the fact the school was situated in the most touristy area of the city with scenic views from my desk (I was spoiled), it definitely was a more relaxed environment than I had anticipated, in that sense, and working each day with such a tightknit and passionate group of people was an element of my co-op that I valued and knew I wanted to find in my future career.

The relaxed and vibrant culture at the company was one that I cherished while I was part of it, but in a sense, took for granted until I began my second co-op at a large corporate, tech headquarters office where the perks outweighed the bad on paper by metric tons, but the passionate culture and genuine friendships between co-workers was absent. At the company, we would constantly get together after work whether it was a nearby establishment or a spa-night at someone's house (the school admin was 90% women). I'm sure these close relationships not only increased the positivity and energy in our workplace, as we all actually enjoyed coming to work each day, but also raised the quality of everyone's work as to not place more strain on someone else's already monstrous workload. While the compensation at the company is notoriously low for some work employees, the experience gained, the friendships made and the overall young and vibrant culture fostered is the reason many stay.

Working at this co-op was not only a fun and exciting experience but a wholesome, developmental one, too. I gained experience in a variety of departments, organizing events, creating partnerships, revising processes. I would have operational tasks each week to complete, and also have monthly or solo projects to develop, too. I value my education with such high regard, but nothing in the

171

classroom can prepare a student for the real world much like a co-op can. I learned how crucial flexibility is, how to balance professionalism in a casual environment, how to live life without naps, and most importantly, what I do and don't value about a company culture and role. I understood how important a friendly and tightknit company culture was to me, and how I want to pursue a career where I positively impact people's lives. In the organization employees can make a direct impact, as I would meet and know the student I was helping, sitting across from me. Yet, I also understood that long-term, I strive to pursue a career that creates a larger positive impact than simply finding host families for affluent internationals learning English. I cherish my learned experiences and would definitely work in a similar school or tour again further down the road, yet it helped me distinguish my career path in a way that traditional classroom learning doesn't even possess.

I had already known I wanted to get more involved in business before this co-op, and the semester before had switched my track from International Affairs to Business so I could transfer in the fall.

All of my courses before this co-op aside from co-op class and Computer Science were not necessary to excel in this position.

I would definitely recommend this to others, and I did when the fall co-op cycle was being hired. However, they offered it to someone who turned down the position, and they couldn't find a replacement co-op in time. Due to this, the role was cut from the budget.

Interviewee #4 of 4

This past January, I began working as a 6-month Member Engagement Co-op. As part of the marketing team, member engagement focuses on pinpointing and producing relevant content that keeps the community involved in not only tracking their own health data and finding support but also in participating in our own research and that of our partners. The young company has kept its startup feel by encouraging employees to take new ideas and "run with them." This was very important to me in my co-op search and aligned perfectly with my interest and educational background in entrepreneurship. I have watched the company grow immensely in the short time that I have been here.

Member engagement adds value to the organization by consistently bringing members back to the site to donate their health data, which in turn contributes to research and efforts toward improving the patient experience. The organization hires co-ops to participate in all branches of the company. While I am the first co-op to join the marketing team, previous co-ops have been hired to work in business development, research, and project management.

The organization has more than doubled in size the past few years to 177 employees and is currently considering finding a new office location to house the many new employees who have joined the company. A complete breakdown of company structure can be found on the website featuring six teams: Consumer & Technology, Research & Informatics, Health, Client Services, Administration & Shared Services, and the Board of Directors. Every employee, even co-ops, is featured with a small bio and link to his or her organization profile. Once again, this highlights the company's value of openness and personal dedication to the patients and community members. Co-ops are treated and valued as full-time employees with the opportunity to work on projects outside our specific positions

As a member engagement co-op, I am both treated as and given the same responsibilities as a full-time member engagement employee. The position includes communication, research, editorial work, and some project management. I am directly responsible for creating communication ideas and campaigns sent out for my assigned conditions. This position is relatively new as we are currently building up and restructuring member communications. Even as a co-op, my opinions are valued, and I can contribute to the development of our new strategies and organization.

At the organization, some of our key goals- aside from putting the patient first- are to improve the patient experience, enable similar patients to connect, empower patients to track their data, provide relevant factual and supportive content to our members, and research cures to the best of our ability. One of the challenges we faced had to be very careful with our choice of language as to not suggest that a patient use a specific treatment but rather spread knowledge and encourage conversation between patients and their doctors. Another challenge was recruiting and providing an incentive for patients with specific conditions to take the time to donate their data and participate in our research.

In the position I have, every day is a little different. Some tasks, such as community health, remain the same. Every morning when I first arrived at the office, I would check the Google alerts I have set to watch for timely news articles concerning those conditions. I then spend time reading through each and thinking about if/how I can use it in a campaign, series, newsletter, or one-off communication. Each condition requires a monthly newsletter as well as 3-4 condition-specific communications. Our team had both weekly and monthly meetings where we brainstorm new ideas, fine-tune existing ideas, update each other on current articles, and decide what communications would be sent out and when.

After getting approval and creating and sending a PowerPoint deck detailing the specifics to my manager, I coordinate with a copywriter and the design team if an infographic is needed. Other than community health, my day is filled with project-specific meetings, ethnographies, and some light data analytics. Member engagement is looped into projects to create member journey maps that identify and describe patient involvement at each step in the process and outline their journey from start to finish. Ethnographies, usual precursors to upcoming projects, are patient, provider, or expert interviews that provide us with insight into the condition we are studying. Data analytics is used to measure the success of past campaigns, series, and communications we have sent out. Using a program called Tableau, our business intelligence team creates both condition-specific and all-encompassing dashboards set to control groups. By analyzing these dashboards, we can identify trends and patterns that aid in creation of future successful communications.

Aside from the tasks assigned to this position, my manager gave me the opportunity to reach out to and work with any other department in the business that I am interested in. Because of this, I have also worked with the research science department, advertising, and the business intelligence team. While working with research science and business intelligence, I had the chance to convert survey and study results into both readable data for my team and tangible givebacks for patients. For advertising, I aided in the creation and monitoring of Facebook ads.

Every task and responsibility of this position as well as most others at the organization involves coordination between two or more teams. As mentioned before, member engagement interacts daily with communications, business development, advertising, design, project coordinating, product, and editing teams. Most meetings for any project have at least one member, if not more, representing each team. The office is very collaborative, and each team is set up in a pod with open desks both standing and sitting.

The technical functions necessary to perform in my position were pretty basic. I needed to know how to use a computer, input data in an Excel sheet, and create presentations. The main skill required specific to this position is the ability to think outside the box.

The projects I worked on required data sensitivity, cultural understanding, and effective communication skills. I had the opportunity to work with patients all over the world and hear their inspiring stories. Academically, the International Business and Organizational Behavior courses I took helped me to understand how people from different parts of the world communicate. Other business and entrepreneurship courses provided me with experience working with and creating business plans. This experience allowed me to better understand and analyze the scope of work we received for every incoming project. When working with the business intelligence team, my courses in statistics proved themselves to be very useful. I was able to interpret and draw my own conclusions from the data we received.

Some projects I worked on were continuous and checked up on daily. A major goal of the position I am in is to keep members engaged and active. If a member is engaged the second month and continues to be active throughout the fifth quarter, the odds of them remaining on the site are far greater. Other goals of projects for this position go hand in hand with engagement. They include recruiting patients for projects and bringing inactive users back to the site.

The most important software for my position was a proprietary software suite. This tool would take all of the data from our site and turns it into interactive graphs, charts, and sets. This is where we can monitor our engagement, monthly sign-ups, click-through rates, social involvement, data donation, and email tests.

After reading through a scope of work for a particular project, I research target patients and begin to develop a customized engagement plan to fit their needs. I am then given the opportunity to sit in for condition ethnographies and listen to the patients themselves describe their experience and tell me what they want. After fine-tuning the engagement plans, I meet with our team to set up a condition-specific dashboard and control group. Throughout the project, I monitored this dashboard to see what communications performed better than others. This data will tell me which formats, content, social vehicle, and presentation work the best with the community we have.

One of my functions at the organization is to create deep-dive content poll reports. After spending time reading through the organization profiles, forum posts, journal entries, the research portal, and messages directly from patients, I would compile the data and information into a PowerPoint deck and present my findings to my team. I used the information I found to develop engagement plans and ideas for series, emails, forum posts, and other campaigns. I also had the opportunity to work on a client presentation for one of the companies we are currently working with. I participated in patient ethnographies where we interviewed condition-specific patients for incoming projects and partnerships.

Everyone at the organization was encouraging and supportive. Anytime I have received an evaluation of my work during a presentation or in an email, my day-to-day advisor has expressed extreme satisfaction and complimented my timeliness, organization, and creativity. I was very proactive with the work I presented and would send rough drafts ahead of time to receive constructive criticism and edit accordingly.

I really enjoyed working for this company because my goals and values align with what it stands for. I have realized that the value of openness and putting patients first is not as common as it should be, but is very important to me and will definitely be something I look for in a future career. I loved my position because of the flexible job description, creativity, and opportunity to work with every other team in the company as well as directly with patients. While member engagement is not a position I considered previous to my co-op, it has sparked an interest, and I hope to have the chance to work in a similar role in the future.

My role in member engagement has made me interested in communications and visual design. I hope to take courses in both as well as continuing to learn by experience.

Courses I took that were most applicable to this position include business statistics, organizational behavior, international business and relations, and global management. A background in business statistics made it easier for me to pull from the raw data we have and apply it to the engagement plans I was developing. Organizational Behavior expanded my communication skills and understanding of the company structure. It also helped me to appreciate the office culture and company as a whole. There were a few specific principles that stuck out and reminded me of topics covered in class including personality and values, motivation, and work/life integration. I believe that the organization is such a great place to work because everyone they bring onboard truly believes in what the company stands for. Because of these common values, people are motivated and more productive. The company is also very flexible with hours and schedules; most people worked from home 1-2 days a week and made it very easy to work remotely. The business management and relations courses focused on the specifics of creating a business plan and cultural communication. This came as a benefit when we reviewed scopes of work and project contracts. It was easier for me to understand each portion of the plans we read. Also, being conscious of different cultural business practices made it easier for me to adapt each engagement plan to the partner we were working with. A few classes that provided me with more soft skills rather than hard skills applicable to my position include math courses other than statistics and economics.

One notable distinction between my education and on-the-job experience was the motivation of my peers. Everyone at the organization wanted to be there and was happy to be working and contributing to the company. This motivation plays a role in the overall experience because it creates a more positive environment and office culture where it is easier to expand and continue to learn. Another distinction is the fact that there is no was right answer when you were on the job. You have to work together with your team continuously to come up with innovative solutions and learn by trial and error, constantly adjusting to your audience's needs. This differed from group projects in courses where some students and peers may be unmotivated to work toward a goal that does not align with their own values.

I do believe that my co-op made good use out of my technical background. A lot of what I did get involved with was working with social media, which is very popular in today's culture. However, the position was more based on creative thinking and coming up with your own engagement plans based on what you read or researched. Some of the hard skills used included creating PowerPoint presentations and doing general research.

I was extremely satisfied with this co-op and would highly recommend it to anyone interested in entrepreneurship, marketing, health, or communications. I felt that I was valued as much as any other employee and everything I contributed actually made a difference. There was always something for me to do and I had the opportunity to work on small projects for other teams as well as my own.

I don't really see a way that this co-op could be improved- it was absolutely perfect for me! Some people may not have liked the position because the team is in the middle of restructuring and redefining our goals. Personally, I loved it because I had the chance to contribute to the new design and flow of work as well as connect with other departments and get their input on the function of my team. This position was very easy to introduce new ideas and run with them.

CHAPTER 8

GETTING EXPERIENCE
AND A FOOT IN THE DOOR

WHICH JOBS APPEAL TO YOU?

It's important to enjoy your work and stay motivated. To achieve this, you'll need to find the right job for you. If you've yet to decide on the career path that you want to follow, a vital step is to narrow your job search. Although a career change further down the line is always possible, making the best choice now will bring you great job satisfaction and help to avoid boredom or stress setting in at a later stage. If you don't know where to begin, take a step back and think about the things that would make up your ideal job. What would you love to do? What are you good at? What are your interests, motivations, and values? What kind of lifestyle do you want? What skills have you developed during your degree study and work experience? Consider what will impress employers, and carry out an audit to identify those qualities and capabilities. As well as revealing where you are already strong, this approach will make you aware of any skills or qualifications you still need to gain to meet the requirements of particular jobs.

There are numerous ways to conduct a skills audit. For example, you can draw up a table that includes the skills you'll need for your future job, a description of these skills, your progress toward gaining them, and evidence of when and where you've demonstrated each one. Another method of finding out about your character traits, strengths and weaknesses are to take psychometric tests. You may have heard of these being used in job interviews, but they can also serve a purpose as a self-assessment tool. They don't require right answers—you just need to respond honestly, and the results will indicate where your strengths lie.

EXPLORE DIFFERENT SECTORS

An essential factor in your job hunt is deciding on the area that you want to work in. For example, would you prefer the relative security of working for a large corporate entity in the private sector? Or do you want to give back to society through public service or charity work? Here are your options:

Private

Encompasses all for profit businesses that aren't run by the government. The main types private sector organizations are sole proprietors, franchises, partnerships, and corporations.

Public

Consists of national and local governments, plus their agencies and chartered bodies. Resources are owned and controlled by the state. The public sector has historically been recognized as offering extensive training, equal opportunities policies, and excellent benefits and pensions.

Charity/Nonprofit

Often referred to as the third sector, the nonprofit sector and the voluntary and community sector. Its priority is to use funds raised to deliver on the charity's particular aims and objectives. Paid and voluntary roles are available.

IDENTIFY EMPLOYERS

Another thing to consider is what type of employer suits your personality and work ethic.

Self-Employment

Covers freelance work, setting up your own business and buying into an existing business. You'll need to be good at networking, making decisions and focusing on achieving your business goals.

Small and Medium-sized Enterprises

Made up of 250 employees or fewer, these are sometimes overlooked by job-hunters, as they don't have the influence or visibility of larger corporations. With a proactive approach and a bit of research, however, you'll find great opportunities. Starting salaries may be lower, but you'll have higher responsibility earlier in your career.

Large Companies

Comprising more than 250 employees, these include many well-known recruiters as well as national and global organizations. Better resources and budgets lean toward higher salaries and support for professional qualifications, but longer hours and less flexibility are also more common.

BEGIN YOUR SEARCH

To get started, make a list of employers that you're interested in working for and check to see if they have any vacancies. Contact companies that you'd like to work for directly, even if they aren't currently advertising any positions. There are some resources for you to use at this point. You can attend graduate fairs, use social media, and visit your university careers service for advice and guidance. When you've focused your search, you should work on your resume and cover letter. These should be tailored to the role you're applying for each time. Read the job description and person specification thoroughly, and then match them to your skills and qualifications.

A Three-Year Plan

I approached the world of work with what I call my 'Three-Year Plan.' When people hear it's a three-year plan, they ask, "What do you mean? You mean you're only going to be there—with a company—for three years?" It should sound that way to some. I would never plan to stay with any organization more than three years. If you do, that's great, but I would never PLAN to do that. I would never go somewhere and say, "I'm going to stay here for the next twenty years no matter what." I think that's ridiculous because with the organization you join today, something could happen or change, beyond your control and it would not be the same organization tomorrow. Just look at what's taken place in many industries and with many companies in the past few years, and you can see that this is true. It will be even more prevalent in the future as companies seek maximum flexibility (which is often at a cost to the employees) to respond to changes in the business and economic environment. It's happened to me a few times in my career. I've gone to work for a great place with a great boss and the next thing I knew, the organization had a leadership change or an organizational strategy change and made the once great place where I worked ... no longer a place for me to stick around.

Year One

Year one is all about discovery! Figure out the organization. They have an overall personality, a culture if you will, just like people. It's important to get a feel for that so you can see how you fit within that framework. You will work hard. Focus on meeting people, networking, growing your brand. Handle some projects and have some wins; your goal is to be seen as a team player and someone who can be counted on.

Year Two

Year two is all about delivery! Deliver, deliver, and deliver. Everything you put your name on, do your best to make sure it is a solid deliverable, a solid product. You are being paid to get results. Never forget this. It is not about being liked at work, it is about being productive and effective. Year two is all about delivering on work, delivering on promises and delivering on building key relationships. Deliver, deliver, and deliver.

Year Three

Year three is all about deciding, and that requires evaluation. Evaluating the work you've done, assess the relationships you've created, gauging whether or not you think you're going to have a future with the organization—and that's probably the most crucial part. Assessing what's next for you with the company and whether or not you have a future starts halfway through year three. By the time year, three has come, you should have worked hard to be known to the organization and to know it in return. You've delivered, you've gotten some wins, and you've built the foundation of a brand.

You also must appraise how those things you've done have impacted the business, hopefully for the better—with some noticeable change in behavior, growth of revenue, saving of dollars, something of that nature—tangible evidence of your benefit to the organization. As you go through this period, you ask yourself, "Do I have a future with this organization? Will this organization sustain my growth? Is there a career path for me here? Are all of these things available to me?" And you need to confirm that with your boss(es), to be sure that they see the same as you. If what you and they believe is all positive about your place and future prospects in the organization then reset the clock. That's what I did if it looked like the situation was working for me, I planned for another three years. Of course, this success comes with circumstances and sacrifices but, as I said earlier if you're not willing to put forth the effort (and make some sacrifices) ... then you really don't want it that bad.

Having A Personal Exit Strategy

This is about self-leadership. It all ties back into defining your core values, determining who you are and your self-worth both individually and as a member (employee, etc.) of an organization. Self-leadership really means self-determination. I'll put here two lines from *Invictus* (by the English poet William Ernest Henley) that you may be familiar with...

I am the master of my fate:
I am the captain of my soul.

You are those things only if you choose to be or set out to be. It's a choice and with it comes the responsibility to act.

There comes a time in your professional career when you are asked to give more of yourself than you may want. It was at that point when I had to decide if I was a 'company man' or if I was more rogue and independent. Are you willing to sacrifice for the long hours, commit to the endless politicking, and are you truly ready to give up a sense of self to 'fit' within the company culture? There is no one-size-fits-all right or wrong answer here; each of us has a choice to make that is distinctly ours.

Usually, your gut will tell you early on if the company is the right fit for you long-term or not. You get a sense of the order of things, the expectations, the unwritten rules and you either decide to assimilate or you rebel.

What you decide is up to you, but the results are not always within your control. If you choose to assimilate, it may be that the organization is not ready to acculturate you and take you into the fold. You may not fit the ideal corporate mold. Read the tea leaves early.

But let's say you are ready to make the commitment, prepared to make a sacrifice, to kneel at the altar of the company... but what if the company is not as committed to you as you thought. Point is you always need an exit strategy—a backup plan—even when things are going great. Even as the company continues to tell you that you're high potential and have a lot of 'headroom' or 'runway' or whatever other *buzzword de jour* is in use to imply, 'stick with us, because you're going places.'

I have watched it happen to too many good people. They get caught up in their own hype, and they overvalue their own stock in the eyes of the organization (remember what I said about conducting a real assessment, honesty starts within). And then it hits, something goes awry; a promotion does not come through, or you are passed over for that great opportunity you were sure was coming your way. And you have not thought about what happens when what you expect doesn't turn out in your favor. What do you do then?

Do not get caught in this situation. Always have options, always have an exit strategy. You never know when you may need it, and to not have one, will leave you caught unaware and blindsided.

LEARNING WHILE EARNING
Who You Show as Yourself Starts on Day One

Interns, Co-ops, New Hires... all are fresh faces, with new ideas and aspirations. All surely plan to work hard to impress their new employer.

So, after a few weeks or months... how have you wowed them? What was your onboarding experience? Did you have one? Or did the company or organization just think it was good enough to give you a job and leave it at that? Let me say that I hope the sentiment is not the latter. Leading effectively often means doing the right thing for all and not just some of the people.

CHAPTER 9

GOING FROM CO-OP TO EMPLOYMENT OFFER

College life can be a fantastic experience for many. It often provides that first taste of independence, experiences that offer new insights into life, and the formation of friendships that last a lifetime. And then comes that day when a student must leave all that behind— graduation.

This is the point where college graduates begin to discover how those years of academic preparation and college experiences pay off in life. It takes more than a college degree to make it in the real world. Employers look for a variety of 'soft' skills to back up the technical training and education you receive in pursuit of your degree.

Learn how to shake a hand, make steady eye contact and dress well for a business event. Attending networking events can help you connect with alumni and professionals in your chosen field. When you attend a networking event, set a goal of having two or three meaningful conversations about your experience and goals for the future.

As you network and make connections, you'll need to know how to draw upon them to build your career. Keep track of the people you've met, how you can help them and how they can help you. Advocate for others, especially when they may be in a position to return the favor. At the same time, be cautious about putting your credibility on the line. As a young professional, you don't have the personal-professional capital to risk vouching for anybody yet.

Strong written communication skills are essential in the real world. Being able to write a clear email or cover letter is a must to get the door open. And yes, engaging in seemingly awkward banter is part of your communication skillset. It's often a key component to building meaningful relationships, introducing yourself to prospective employers, getting to know team members and finding success at networking events. Instead of asking what someone does at work, make your questions more specific. And when someone asks you a question, give an interesting answer, tell them a story in the context of your achievements.

Many potential employers will assume that you have the skills to interact professionally with customers, write effectively and work within a team. The real-world skill they often lack is the ability to identify an employer's challenges and offer a workable solution. What employers want to hear about is how you can solve their business problems.

To get to the corner office, you need to do your homework. How? Discover an employer's business problems and come to the interview armed with solutions. As younger employees may struggle to see the reasons why things are the way they are, at a new employer and can get frustrated. To counter that, focus on the big picture. "Think of yourself as a researcher as you examine businesses or companies. Ask yourself why they do things the way they do, what are industry standards, how does the corporate strategy translate to the person at the lowest ranks." Doing so can help you understand the soft skills and social norms you need to follow within the company.

CARVING OUT YOUR PATH

CEOs, Boards of Directors, and Business Owners now—since the recession of 2008 that has lingered for years—think a little bit differently, at least the smart ones do. They are trying to find out, "How do I build a strong, stable organization that will perform well year in, year out, no matter what's going on? How do I develop or find personnel with talent that gives me that agility, that flexibility to adapt." You can't do it with one person if you put them in the scenario we sketched out previously, where person and culture don't mesh. They could be the most intelligent person on the planet—but if you don't have the right pieces and support around them, leaders that makes the business work; then you cannot be a repeat champion, you cannot sustain performance. It's foolishly betting everything on one person's abilities. And that's not smart on any level.

ASK FOR ADVICE

An appointment to talk with a career advisor should be your first stop. They can help you to identify areas of interest as well as opportunities, as they have often spent many years forging strong relationships with companies locally, nationally and internationally and may be able to give you the head start that you need. Look into any internship, and co-op programs run by your institution, as the experience will be of high quality, with a particular focus on adding value to the student.

USE YOUR CONTACTS

Many students feel that they don't have any connections, but this is rarely the case. You should consider existing networks; enquiring about opportunities with family, friends, and colleagues can yield impressive results. You can also create your own networks through social media, or by joining a professional body. Using existing contacts is a great way to find any type of work experience, and you should get comfortable with using LinkedIn.

LOOK ONLINE

It may seem obvious, but the internet can provide a wealth of opportunities if you look in the right places. Regularly check company websites, as openings can appear without warning. Social media is also incredibly useful. Not only is it a great way to search for placements but also employers could directly approach you if you have a strong and professional online appearance. Use caution when searching online as there are plenty of websites out there, but you really need to be aware of unpaid internships and the quality of the experience on offer.

APPLY SPECULATIVELY

Not all internships are advertised, especially those in smaller companies or in sectors such as the media. A speculative approach involves identifying and contacting a potential employer to ask about opportunities. It's vital to do your research and target the organization and role. Don't be afraid of this approach. Focus your application on what you can offer the company and showcase the enthusiasm that you have for the position.

Once you've secured work experience, it's vital that you don't waste the opportunity.

APPLY THE CO-OP LESSONS LEARNED

Here's how to make it count. Before your first day, it's a good idea to research the company's interests, their current projects and any plans they have. Your supervisor will welcome having a good understanding of where you fit into the bigger picture.

GET INVOLVED

Work experience is your chance to discover whether a job is right for you, and the best way to find out is by talking to people. Show staff members that you want to learn and take responsibility. Find out about the people you work with, ask about their roles and see if you can gain experience in that area. Every boss values someone who is willing to help others with their workload.

MANAGE YOUR WORKLOAD

There's no point asking for extra work if you don't have the time to do it. Make sure that you manage your time effectively and stick to any deadlines you're given. Whether you write to-do lists, put reminders in your diary or use post-it notes, you need to find techniques that work for you. Blocking out time to complete tasks can help you not get distracted and spend too much time on any one item on your list. Everyone works at different speeds so getting your workload right may take time. Don't wait to be given work. Tell your supervisor if you are ready for more, as they may be worried to give you too much.

MASTER THE BASICS

If you don't get the basics right and turn up on time, you'll undermine any great work that you've done. Avoid being late at all costs. If you're going to be late due to exceptional or unforeseen circumstances, ensure you telephone your supervisor to let them know. Turning up late won't make a great impression—but neither will only doing 9am to 5pm. Don't start work precisely on the start time and finish exactly on the finish time. If you see any teammates working long hours, ask them if there is anything you can do to help.

There are basic skills that all who enter the workforce need, but specifically in business they can be more important than just a grounding or entry-level proficiency. And these, if you focus on first developing a solid foundation, can be looked at through a different lens so that you can hone them to the point where you can put your own twist on them. And when you can do that the 'authentic' you will shine through.

CHAPTER 10

USING CAREER COACHING TO YOUR ADVANTAGE

Career coaching helps people find greater fulfillment in their careers by establishing professional goals, creating a plan and overcoming obstacles that may be in the way.

Career coaches can help people with a wide array of career-related issues. Some seek assistance because they're 'stuck on start' in a job that brings little meaning or purpose; while others are challenged by the demands of balancing their work and personal lives. Some clients know exactly what they want to do with their careers, but need help finding and executing a plan to get there, while others struggle without identifying a clear calling or purpose. Career coaching can help you with all of these concerns and more.

WHAT ARE THE BENEFITS OF HAVING A CAREER COACH?

Clearly, the most important benefit is that a career coach supports you along your way. They actively listen to what you are saying and what you aren't saying. They will create a safe environment where you are comfortable and can talk without judgment. Deciding on what to do in your career can be incredibly isolating, and it can often become paralyzing. Working with a career coach provides you with the necessary support to move forward. A coach offers non-judgmental guidance and sees things from an objective point of view, which enables them to offer different perspectives and identify opportunities. They'll help you recognize where you are stuck, what the obstacles are between you and your dream job, and illuminate the path leading to what you really want.

They do this by setting up regular career meetings with you (virtually or in person) and assist in developing a plan to achieve your career goals. Finding your next job can be frustrating, annoying and demoralizing and it may be difficult to know where to start. And sometimes even good starts lead to dead ends. Having regular coaching sessions will lend structure and stability to your career transition. A career coach will customize a program to suit your individual needs that fit with where you are today or in the future, whether at a career crossroad or in job search mode. Career coaches will provide the necessary accountability for you to achieve and exceed your goals, far faster than you would on your own.

Targeted career coaching will help you focus on what you really want to do and where you want to do it by identifying your values, interests, talents, and passion. They will help you discover what is really important to you and how that relates to finding your ideal career path determined by a new awareness of your strengths, accomplishments, unique value proposition and your own personal brand.

How Does Career Coaching Work?

On one end of the spectrum is the personal development side that helps you answer the big questions in life such as, 'What are you passionate about?' What do you really want to do? And what career legacy do you want to leave behind?

On the other end is the professional development side with work on such items as resume writing, LinkedIn profile review, preparing for interviews, and developing job search skills. A career coach can provide assistance if you are currently employed and looking to make a transition into another industry or job or if you are re-entering the workforce. They can help you find direction when you lack focus and don't know what your next steps are. Whether you want to start a new career, or are a new graduate fresh out of college or university seeking your first job, or are hoping to find fulfillment in a current career path, a career coach can help ease the transition and get you where you want to go faster with less stress.

Career coaching is similar in nature to career counseling. The difference—an important one—is that a counselor provides you with industry information and advice to help you find a job. A career coach goes deeper to look at your whole life, to help you find what fits your passion. A career counselor takes an educational, directive approach to building your tools for acquiring a job. They help you assess the current employment landscape by providing employment information such as industry trends, employment statistics, salary expectations, and more. They also provide tactical support to find a job. For example, they can help you refine your resume, write a compelling cover letter, and get the interview. This may be what you are looking for, especially if you are new to the workforce and are seeking an entry-level position.

While similar in many ways, career coaching focuses more on your personal strengths, talents, and values, and helps you build your ideal career path based on these fundamental factors. A career coach works with you to find your true calling in the workplace, the career that will give you real meaning and purpose. Career coaching is based on the premise that if you are going to spend eight hours a day or more in your job, it might as well be something that you love.

A career coach will take the time to really listen to you and uses a variety of tools, exercises, and activities to help you identify your career goals and, critically, take action toward achieving them. After only a few sessions, you will have a much clearer sense of what type of career that will give you the most joy and satisfaction, at which point you'll be in the position to start developing an action plan to get there.

WHAT ARE THE PROS AND CONS?

Pros

One major pro of a good career coach is they have no preconceived opinions and will be able to take you through a deep-dive of your entire life helping you uncover your true natural gifts are while discovering what it is that brings you the greatest fulfillment. Once you have a better understanding of who you truly are and what makes your heart sing, you will gain tremendous clarity on your true purpose—what you are meant to be doing on this earth. At that point, a skilled career coach can help you get beyond what you see (about yourself and job breaks) to show you what you should see (and what opportunities are truly out there). Which can be an eye-opening process on its own.

What's more, you also have the benefit of having someone with the knowledge and experience to help guide you through the process. To take this a step further, an experienced career coach will teach you how to listen to your own inner voice and discover what really makes you happy. I find people spend a lot of time and money attempting that and often don't figure it out alone. What I have discovered after years coaching many people in their career pursuits is that, if you learn to listen to your heart, your inner wisdom, you will find what you need to be more professionally satisfied. And that joy can be found if you focus on growing what has been discovered in your personal deep-dive and looking at what your potential is with your career coach.

On the technical side, career coaches are there to support and encourage you when you become disheartened or face setbacks. Career coaches are experienced in knowing what employers look for and how you can better represent yourself on your resume, cover letter, and in a job interview. They help you clear your roadblocks and identify what might be keeping you stuck. They will help you gain the confidence and skills to move forward in the direction you are meant to go and can help you balance your current life needs with your career goals. And last but not least, career coaches are the ultimate sounding boards and will hold you accountable (a true requisite) so you can make progress.

Cons

One of the drawbacks of hiring a coach is the expense. But consider this: your career and happiness should be treated as an essential investment. Although it is understandable that financial limitations are sometimes unavoidable. If you do not have any disposable income or cannot enlist the help of friends and family to help you pay for these services, it will be difficult.

Another con is the challenge of finding the right coach. One who can honestly do what they say and help you move forward. How do you know if they are right? How do you know if they can help you make those game-changing, life-changing breakthroughs? Are they a coach who can help you discover your own wisdom or will they force their beliefs and biases on you? You want someone who is listening to you and your innermost interests and not pushing what they think is best for you. This comes back to you really knowing yourself.

After having your first conversation with a potential coach, take time to reflect and ask yourself, is this person right for me? Will this person help me take my life to a much better place? See if you get a positive response such as a clearer mind, a sigh of relief, a new smile on your face, or just a good feeling when you think about starting this journey with a career coach. If so, then it's like your green light to explore further or move forward with them. If instead, all that you get are questions or worries or anxiety, there is a reason for that. Listen to it. Don't proceed. Your mind and heart know what's best for you, all you have to do is listen to them.

ARE YOU READY TO HIRE A CAREER COACH?

Here's what you need to know to find the right coach specifically for you. Hiring a coach to assist and support you in your career can be one of the wisest investments you'll make in today's ever-changing world of work. Depending on your needs, you might find that coaching is your bridge to more motivation and fulfillment on the job, better performance (and recognition), to a brand-new career or to navigating your way through a tough job search. But how do you know when it's time to work with a coach or how to go about finding one who will be a good match for you and your goals? What you need—and want—from a coach has a lot to do with where you're at in your career. Are you just starting out? Looking to transition out of a dead-end job into more meaningful work? In love with your profession, but feeling burned out in your current role? Ready to move up the ladder in your organization or to leave and join another similar company? Maybe you've achieved your goals, and you're ready to use your experience and skills in a whole new way. Perhaps you're coming back into the workforce, but you're not sure what you want to do.

If you find yourself in any of the above situations and haven't worked out a resolution on your own, it's time to consider getting a career coach. Understanding yourself will help you choose a coach whose approach and methodology is a good fit for you. If you needed to find a job immediately, your strategy—and potentially the coach you choose—may be a lot different than if you're employed and contemplating a transition into more meaningful work. Long-term goals, such as identifying your career path or finding what's next for you, require time to explore your options and dig deep into who you are, what you're great at and what kind of work and lifestyle are important to you. Short-term goals such as refining your resume or improving your job search strategy may or may not play into your long-term career goals. Coaching is a partnership designed to support you, challenge you, and hold you accountable as you develop and achieve your career goals and vision. While your coach will offer valuable assessments, tools and assignments, resources and a safe, confidential sounding board, it's up to you to choose where you want to focus. You'll get the most from your investment when you're prepared to fully engage, put new ideas into action and use the support and accountability of a coach to your benefit.

SOME THINGS TO CONSIDER

Career Direction

A career coach can help you identify your ideal career and understand what the right career fit is for you long-term, so you are no longer job hopping and wondering why you can't find what's right for you. But before hiring a career coach, ask yourself what your career direction is currently. What do you want it to be? Do you want to work in the same industry, or work in a different capacity, or do you like what you do but maybe just in a different place? Although career coaches can help you to know yourself better, it's best to have a general idea of where you would like to see yourself in the future. This will also help you to identify if the coach has the right knowledge and experience to get you to where you want to be.

Work Performance

Career coaches can enable you to become a top performer through education, accountability, and guidance on change management, time management, building confidence, on becoming a better manager, and much more. Again, identifying what or exploring areas of your current job you could improve on. If nothing comes to mind, ask your boss to schedule an employee review, or ask a trusted fellow employee. These areas of work performance are critical to job success, and many of us aren't as proficient in some areas as we would like to be. Knowing your weaknesses is key to eliminating or mitigating their impact and will be something a good coach will address with you.

Personalized Self-Assessment & Discovery

Be honest with your potential career coach about what you hope to gain and ask them how they would personalize your experience. On a first call, a career coach won't have enough personal information about you to do the deep-dive discussed earlier, but an experienced coach should be able to provide a generalized idea of how they would tailor their program to your needs.

Development of Clear Direction & Specific Plan

Ask your potential coach for a breakdown of their plan detailing how they work with clients. Ask them what specific tools they use to help their clients reach their goals. Have them explain their ideas for career opportunities in your industry.

Develop Skills, Tools & Confidence

To execute your plan, a career coach should help you develop skills, tools, and confidence including communication, management of time and resources, emotional intelligence for personal effectiveness, visioning, planning, identifying strengths and weaknesses, understanding and communicating your vision, mission and brand. Ask your potential coach for a few past success stories in this area. You could ask them something like, "Could you tell me about a former client who struggled with confidence and how you helped them to feel more successful?"

Remember as good as a coach is—no matter their success with other clients—you will be principally responsible for the success of their program. Although a career coach can have a great plan and be very experienced, they can't do the work for you. You have to be prepared to invest the time into the exercises and assignments. Ask your prospective coach how much time they would expect you to spend on their assignments per week. But remember, having a career coach is much more than just accountability. It is an investment in your most important asset... you! And this investment pays off handsomely if it helps you avoid being 'stuck on start' as you move from campus to corner office.

WHY CAREER COACHING WORKS

Awareness

This is about helping you as the client become aware of the key behaviors that either help or hinder their progress and growth. We can't change what we're not aware of, so cultivating awareness in the client for how they show up and what they can do differently is crucial.

Alignment

Career coaching works best when there is alignment with what you want to work on and what is significant to the organization. It is also important to have buy-in and involvement from a sponsor such as a direct boss or human resources representative, so there is a common understanding of the focus of the coaching as well as internal support for the process.

Action

Creating clear goals and a written action plan will help provide you with a road map for achieving the vision for the future. The plan also provides a baseline for the current state, pre-coaching, and indicates progress toward the desired state post-coaching.

Accountability

Coaching by design creates the conditions for you to take responsibility for your growth and provides built-in accountability because the coach will check in on the progress you are making toward agreed-upon action items from the last coaching session.

Acceleration

Clarity of goals support you in overcoming obstacles, align the focus of the coaching, and are the backbone of a written action plan. Having a committed career coach who helps you craft that plan and that holds you accountable, can significantly accelerate the pace in which a client achieves results. Often challenges faced for many months or even years, that you have been unable to address on your own are resolved much quicker and with better results when a coach is involved. This is the power of career coaching in action.

ARE YOU STUCK ON START?

It is no surprise that you continue to grow and change as an individual, especially in an ever-changing world. However, if you want to truly optimize your career path, you must focus on what's important, and what you can control.

As you embark on your career, it's important to empower yourself with a plan using the best-in-class techniques to get an edge over your competition. By avoiding the pitfalls others have already gone through, you will be able to proactively manage your career as it is not a one-time decision but a series of decisions made over your lifetime.

Most people are new to career coaching and may wonder, "what is career coaching?" and "how can a career coach help me?" So, let's look at what the CareerSOS™ Platform is and how it can help you. To get started, consider these seven deep-dive questions:

1. How do you feel about your career?
2. Do you love going to work?
3. Do you feel you've reached your full potential?
4. Are you appropriately compensated for the job you do?
5. Do you feel there is something better for you out there?
6. Do you have both short-term and long-term career goals?
7. Is your career in alignment with your values?

How to Get Unstuck

We all have our basic needs, and for many of us that includes doing well by our family and being able to provide them with a comfortable life. But when thinking about your own purpose in what you do, don't simply stop there. There's more under the surface than that, it may be self-empowerment, it may be about helping others, it may be about fulfilling a desire to learn and to be intellectually challenged, or about introducing new ideas into the world. A targeted set of offerings can be found on the Stuck On Start Coaching website.

CareerSOS™ Monthly Subscription for 'The Focused'

Monthly set up tools, tactics, and targeted advice each month. Your subscription includes career coaching videos twice a month that focus on the 'how' of career navigation, and access to a closed LinkedIn group for those truly focused on a successful career journey. Career Coaching From $1 A Day™.

CareerSOS™ Strategy Sessions for 'The Motivated'

An in-person three-hour strategy session: a proprietary and personalized approach combining not just the latest theory, but practical application and tactics to provide a career action plan that is personalized and a thorough understanding of your goals to help you deliver on your career success.

CareerSOS™ Insider Coaching for 'The Committed'

Depending on your goals, you will break down your plan into actionable steps for each week. You and your career coach will typically meet on a monthly basis to assess your progress, share best practices, and provide guidance on meeting your objectives.

Career coaching can be delivered in many different ways, but the most effective way is one-on-one where you are in a relaxed, private environment. This can be done in person, by phone, or through an online—virtual—meeting platform.

When you're making a career transition, you should focus on what really matters—how to set yourself up for long-term success. Ease the career change by seeking out people who can advise and coach you along the way with perspectives that are different than your own.

Find a career coach who will help you grow—and ultimately help you prepare for the opportunity that will lead to your future success. Are you ready for that? Are you ready to put your career into true focus, to become motivated, and ready to commit to owning your future? Are you ready to not be 'stuck on start' in your career? Learn more at WWW.STUCKONSTARTCOACHING.COM ... Career Coaching From $1 A Day™.

WHY YOU MAY NEED A CAREER COACH EVEN IF YOU ALREADY HAVE A JOB

Many people dismiss the idea of working with a coach because they are already employed. Frequently, many business professionals feel that a career coach is for people who are unemployed and looking for work. But really, helping with resumes and an effective job search are just some of the lesser aspects that job or career coaches help with.

Career coaches also work with business professionals who are already employed. Their objective is to help their clients reach their full potential in their careers. Whether you are currently employed or not, just starting off in your career or a seasoned professional, there are great benefits to meeting with a career coach. For example, perhaps you currently have a job, but you would like to know how to make a long-term career of it. Or maybe you are feeling unhappy with your current job and wondering what you can do about it. Or it's possible you would like to know how to more effectively network in your industry or advance to the next level in your career. A career coach could help you with these situations.

Increasing Responsibility

Maybe you've had the same job for some time and would like to advance in your career. Are you unsure of how to approach your boss or what steps you can take to show you are ready for more responsibility? Through a system of education and accountability, a career coach can help you become a top performer. They can provide guidance on change management, time management, building confidence, becoming a better manager, and much more. They can assess your current process for networking and help you better your approach. They can also examine your professional social media profiles and make sure you are representing yourself in the best way possible. These are examples of facets that are critical to career success, and to be honest, many of us aren't as good in these areas as we could be. Sessions with a career coach can make you a better employee and a better professional. This, in effect, boosts your brand and standing within your industry.

Difficult Situations at Work

Career coaches can also help you prepare for difficult situations or conversations at work. Perhaps you have to talk to your boss about an important, possibly sensitive, issue but are not sure how to bring it up. Or you face a difficult situation with a fellow co-worker and don't know the best way to handle it while keeping a professional relationship with them. During coaching sessions, a career coach can hold practice sessions with you as you act out possible scenarios and responses to help you feel comfortable with whatever reaction you may face. They can help you improve your communication skills to avoid uncomfortable situations in the future, as well as conversations to avoid.

Finding Career Balance

Career coaches can also help you find a happy balance between your work and personal life. Perhaps you are having trouble creating boundaries to keep your personal and business life separate. A coach can help you discover and maintain your priorities in life to feel success in your career and still happy when you leave the office. Perhaps you are unsure how much information is appropriate to share with co-workers during work hours, or what are relevant topics of conversation. A coach will help you understand how to be authentic without being too transparent. This involves learning more about yourself and how to project yourself positively at work while keeping a balance between being overly personal and being too removed emotionally.

Creating A Path to the Corner Office

Unhappiness is actually quite a common problem with employed business professionals. Recent studies show that over 50% of Americans are unhappy at work. You may love the career you chose but currently, don't enjoy your work situation. Many feel that it's as simple as looking for another job when they don't enjoy their job. But many times, they don't stop to analyze the real underlying issues, which makes it harder to find the right fit for them. This is where having a career coach can really prove beneficial.

A career coach can help you discover what success means to you and what action steps you can take to make your work more enjoyable. They can help you identify what to do to make your job more fulfilling. Many times, those who work with a career coach find that a drastic change isn't needed because their coach helped them identify what factors were stopping them from loving their career. Often with small adjustments and guidance, business professionals are able to rekindle their love for their job.

If you find yourself in a situation where you need a career coach, know this: select one that has established a successful professional career before becoming a career coach (and you should check and confirm this). True knowledge comes from vast experience in the business world, they will use theirs to help you become successful.

Conclusion

10 Reasons Co-ops Rock

1. Cooperatives are DEMOCRATIC businesses & organizations EQUALLY OWNED & CONTROLLED by a group of people. There are worker co-ops, consumer co-ops, producer co-ops, financial co-ops, housing co-ops, and more. In a cooperative, ONE member has ONE vote.

2. Because cooperatives are democratically owned by community members, co-ops keep MONEY & JOBS in their communities.

3. Cooperatives aren't a far off theory. Cooperatives offer achievable and practical solutions to many ECONOMIC, ENVIRONMENTAL & SOCIAL PROBLEMS that can be implemented RIGHT NOW.

4. COOPERATIVES AREN'T CHARITY; they're an empowering means for self-help & solidarity.

5. Members equally share THE BURDEN IN HARD TIMES & equally share THE BENEFITS IN GOOD TIMES.

6. Cooperatives are more resilient IN ECONOMIC DOWNTURNS & IN IMPOVERISHED COMMUNITIES. When other businesses may shut down or lay off workers, co-op members pull together TO WORK OUT SOLUTIONS.

7. Cooperatives are an INTERNATIONAL MOVEMENT. There are thousands upon thousands of cooperatives around the world that are making major differences GLOBALLY & LOCALLY.

8. Cooperatives strive to make people's LIVES, COMMUNITIES, AND ECONOMIES more JUST, EQUITABLE, & DEMOCRATIC.

9. There's no one right way to do a co-op. They can be flexible to fit DIFFERENT COMMUNITY & INDIVIDUAL NEEDS. There are big co-ops with thousands of members, and there are small co-ops with only three members.

10. Cooperatives are VIABLE & JUST ALTERNATIVES for meeting our social and economic needs in contrast to CORPORATIONS THAT EXPLOIT the people and the planet.

Brought to you with love & solidarity by
www.

Design by Molly McLeod

210

MOVING INTO THE CORNER OFFICE

As I mentioned previously, being your authentic self is important. There's a maxim—almost universal across professions—that before you break the rules (something all truly 'authentic' and innovative people do), you must understand them at their most complex level.

Skills That Employers Look for and Want

The increasingly overcrowded nature of today's graduate market has made honing your transferable skills more important than ever. Luckily, internships, part-time jobs, co-ops, volunteering, societies and more, can help you prove that you've gained the qualities needed to succeed in the workplace. So, what are employers seeking when it comes to critical skills, and what attributes do you need to impress? Here are five that are commonly sought by recruiters:

(1) Analytical thinking

Many jobs require employees who can gather relevant information, compare data from different sources, and spot trends, associations, and cause-effect relationships.

Grappling with complex information and communicating it effectively to others is a core skill that's relevant to any working environment. Analytical qualities can be developed naturally during the essay-writing process.

You can also grow these skills practically through research-focused part-time work, such as in a museum or library, or through summer internships in roles that require the analysis and manipulation of large datasets.

Being able to identify critical issues and solve them by thinking laterally is also important.

(2) Communication

Strong verbal and written communication skills are essential for all first job out of college roles, but especially those that are business-related. Students must, therefore, demonstrate that they can use language accurately and appropriately, understand others' reactions and feelings, and give clear and persuasive presentations. Verbal communication skills can be developed through voluntary or part-time work in sectors where team objectives and customer satisfaction are the focus. Your writing and speaking skills can be improved through university societies by, for example, inviting guest speakers to events or writing articles for the student newspaper. Strong levels of teamwork are also important. You must show that you work effectively with a diverse range of people, as this is a requirement of all after campus positions. You must also learn how to listen patiently to others, state personal opinions tactfully, and support colleagues' ideas and decisions.

Seek opportunities to present to audiences. Part-time work—including bar, retail, and hospitality roles—provide excellent chances to develop relationship-building skills through interaction with team members and customers.

(3) Flexibility

First jobs are often fast-paced, requiring employees to adapt quickly to changing roles and environments. This makes working well under pressure vital. Recruiters usually want their applicants to display flexibility due to the changing requirements of the business. Impress employers by showing that you can take on new tasks at short notice, are resilient during difficult times, and can stay focused when plans or priorities change. Seeking out challenging opportunities will help you to demonstrate this while providing the added bonus of proving to employers that you are happy to study/work beyond the expected.

Consider applying for a summer internship or a placement abroad as part of your course. This demonstrates to employers that you're willing and able to adapt to different circumstances without your usual support network around you.

(4) Organization

Recruiters frequently require applicants to be organized as graduate roles often involve a range of conflicting priorities and tasks. They also need you to manage yourself, your resources and your colleagues effectively. This means that you must demonstrate to employers that you can plan to deadlines, organize the resources necessary and prioritize tasks logically. You can develop these skills across everyday life by planning your university coursework and exam revision while balancing part-time work and social commitments. Becoming a project planner in your group work also gives you the chance to develop techniques in this area. Extended trips abroad, through volunteering, for example, require organization regarding planning, budgeting, and risk assessment. Employers are looking for people who are organized and commercially minded, and graduates could illustrate this by taking a gap year. These experiences require a lot of drive, energy, and motivation to get off the ground, which can demonstrate your ability to develop beyond academic study.

(5) Enthusiasm

This isn't strictly a skill, but all employers want fun and enthusiastic employees.

Recruiting an employee takes investment (time, resource and financial), so employers want to make sure the candidate is committed to the company. Candidates can demonstrate their enthusiasm by researching the organization and finding out about the culture and values of the company. It's therefore vital that you keep abreast of industry developments by reading the relevant trade press. There is no set route when looking for an internship—in fact, the more ways you approach it, the higher your chances of success. A student should approach the search for an internship precisely as they would a job search. Just like when looking for a job, it pays to be well informed. So do some initial research and talk to people in your sector, whether via social media or in-person at recruitment fairs and insight days. The first step to searching for an internship is knowing what you want to explore in a job. The most prepared for the journey to the corner office think about what they want to get out of the placement, when and where they are able to do it and the structure of what is on offer.

A FINAL WORD

If you've read this book, then you must want to reach a level of success that many college students or recent college graduates don't think about. There is a level of responsibility, risk, and reward that comes with making it to the top of an organization or with making it as an entrepreneur, leading your own company.

The 'key' to the corner office is taking time at the start of your career to prepare for your arrival at that destination. That's why it's important to control your own destiny. Do your homework, work diligently on your preparation. Set up conditions to work in your favor by showing up with the right preparation for the right opportunity. And when you get the opportunity, you will be ready to deliver on arrival!

College should be a fun and enjoyable experience, and that fun experience comes from not spending every moment in a classroom or studying. Co-ops and internships are a way to pay for college other than coming from affluent parents, getting academic or athletic scholarships, or taking out large loans year over year.

If you will commit to maximizing your earning while being focused on the hands on learning during your co-op and internship experience, then you won't be 'stuck on start' in your first few years out of college. You will instead be ready to start your journey from campus to corner office having practiced using your knowledge, skills, and abilities to help you win in the workplace.

ABOUT THE AUTHOR

CURTIS L. ODOM, ED.D.

Dr. Curtis Odom is President of Stuck On Start Coaching, a boutique career coaching firm serving the needs of recent college graduates, and early career professionals by providing customized client offerings under their CareerSOS™ Platform which is designed for anyone feeling "stuck on start" in their current job, and in need of a personal career strategy.

Curtis is also Principal and Managing Partner of Prescient Strategists, a Boston-based, management consulting practice to Fortune 100 companies, colleges, and universities focused on developing and delivering change management, organizational culture, executive coaching, and leadership development solutions to clients during mergers and acquisitions, and strategic business transformation initiatives.

Curtis has built an impressive career having spent 20 years as an internationally acclaimed business leader, entrepreneur, consultant, practitioner, researcher, best-selling author, executive coach, and professor at the Northeastern University D'Amore-McKim School Of Business in Boston, Massachusetts. This experience is preceded by a 10-year active duty military career served proudly in the United States Navy.

As a testament to his professional brand, Curtis was honored internationally as the Post-Merger Integration Advisor of The Year (USA) for 2016 by Corporate LiveWire. Local to Boston, Curtis was also awarded the high distinction of being selected as a member of the Boston Business Journal's Top 40 Under 40 class for 2010.

Curtis is the author of *Mind The Gap: Getting Business Results in Multigenerational Organizations, Generation X Approved: Top 20 Keys to Effective Leadership* as well as the wildly successful *Stuck in the Middle: A Generation X View of Talent Management*. This book, *From Campus to Corner Office: How Co-Ops and Internships Will Help You Win in the Workplace,* is his fourth.

Curtis's articles, interviews, blog postings, and excerpts from his published books have been featured online in *Entrepreneur, Inc., Today.com, Fortune, The Wall Street Journal, The Huffington Post, CNBC, Ebony, The Globe and Mail, Training Magazine,* and in numerous other print and online publications.

CPSIA information can be obtained
at www.ICGtesting.com
Printed in the USA
FFOW02n0416280318
46077903-47031FF